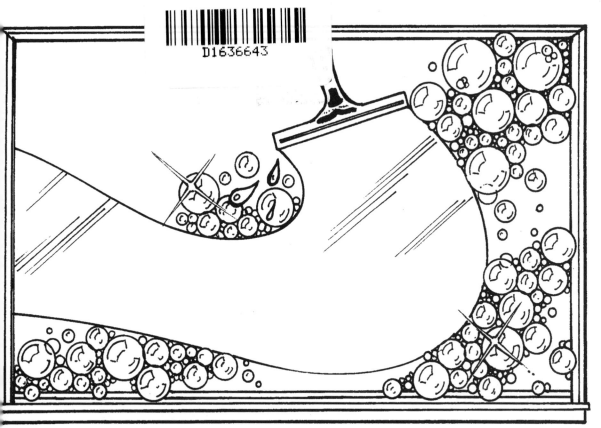

THE *Professional* CLEANER'S *Personal* HANDBOOK

BY DON ASLETT

America's #1 Cleaning Expert

Published by Marsh Creek Press,
PO Box 700, Pocatello, ID 83204;
208-232-3535

ISBN 0-937750-11-5

MARSH CREEK PRESS

Illustrator: Kerry Otteson
Editor: Carol Cartaino
Production: Virginia Cotter
Production Manager: Tobi Haynes
Readers: Jim Doles
        Dana Zimmerman

Also by Don Aslett

Business Books:

Cleaning Up for a Living

How to Upgrade & Motivate Your Cleaning Crew

Check Up—Achieving Quality Control in Cleaning

How to be #1 With Your Boss

*Everything I Needed to Know About Business
I Learned in the Barnyard*

Is There a Speech Inside You?

Cleaning Books:

Is There Life After Housework?

Do I Dust or Vacuum First?

Make Your House Do the Housework

Don Aslett's Clean in a Minute

Who Says It's a Woman's Job to Clean?

Painting Without Fainting

500 Terrific Ideas for Cleaning Everything

Pet Clean-Up Made Easy

How Do I Clean the Moosehead?

Don Aslett's Stainbuster's Bible

The Cleaning Encyclopedia

Painting Without Fainting

Wood Floor Care

Organization & Decluttering:

The Office Clutter Cure

Not for Packrats Only

Clutter's Last Stand

TABLE OF CONTENTS

Preface

A disclaimer... but if I can ever help

INTRODUCTION

PART ONE

PART TWO

A Pro Cleaner's Digest:
HOW TO DO IT

YOU—a Professional!

Being a professional means more than gaining a position and money in a field of expertise. A true professional has an inner instinct for her or his work, wears it in her/his whole being, and is a joy to behold in action.

One day I watched two boxcar loads of yearling cattle pour from the train to the corral in fast-moving and milling mass hysteria. A keen-eyed cattle man, who just arrived and had never seen these cows before, squinted and watched for a few minutes. Then he turned to the official and said, "I'd say 255 head, 373 lbs. apiece." Most of the cowboys looking on might be able to tell you

within 50 cows, how many, or within 40 pounds, how much they weighed. When the tally from the scales and the ledger came, there were 252 cows and they weighed an average of 374.5 lbs. The cattleman was right on—**he was a professional.**

My friend taking his car down to sell it told me of twelve "secret" hidden things wrong with it that the dealer would never know. He pulled it onto the lot, and the dealer slowly walked around it just once. Then he rattled off all twelve, plus two more

things wrong with it. The dealer knew cars so well that just by sound, tilt, tire wear, exhaust color, paint surface, etc., he was able to identify anything amiss. **He was a professional.**

A mother of six was in the midst of a hive of activity. Four of her children had friends over, and she was doing at least five things at once. But suddenly she

stopped, called upstairs, and told the three-year old to put the toothpaste up. She couldn't see him, she just knew by feel and experience what two and a half minutes of silence meant! **She was a professional.**

For years I ran a large hay baler with two loud motors, a hammering plunger, and 32 pulleys all working at once. In the back, near where the bales came out, was a clever set of cog fingers that quietly tied on the soft twine that held the bale together. I became so aware and interpretive of that machine that despite all that racket I could *hear* when the twine didn't hold a knot. **I was a professional.**

Imagine now, as professional cleaners, getting *that* good at what we do. So skilled, so aware that we can feel "clean," can sense every need of the client and the corridors, can clean a bathroom so well it throbs, can tell at a glance what is right or wrong, what's worst or best for our customers, our bosses, and ourselves; can identify by a quick sniff or feel what a stain or spill is, know when a vacuum motor or a belt slips even a bit, can tell by a fleeting expression or eyebrow movement how satisfied our customers are. We can get *that* good at cleaning and when we do, we can wear "professional" as part of our very person, not just a label. What a day that will be, **for you. You're a professional!**

A DISCLAIMER...

(but if I can ever help...)

99% percent of the instructions, information, examples, advice, and suggestions in this book should agree with and complement your own particular cleaning organization and situation. There might be a few places where your company policy requires something different, something more or less. If and when in doubt, be sure to follow your company's and boss's directives first. *Obey the laws, rules, practices, and guidelines of those who employ you.*

I haven't, nor can I ever, cover 100% of the needs and knowledge of the cleaning industry, so this work is condensed and selected down to what I feel is the most important. You may find material here you'd like to copy, use, and share in your own training programs, speeches, presentations, etc. I've purposely kept the price of the book low at $10. And you can get an even lower price by buying a quantity, just call my office. This book is copyrighted; however, as long as you aren't selling it, go ahead and use a page or two—just be sure to invlude the copyright and give the author (me!) a little acknowledgment at the bottom of the page.

INTRODUCTION

We already know each other, because we've done the same kind of work for years. We may not have learned each other's names yet, but boy do we know each other's job! We're both in the cleaning business, professionals at it. It's been 38 straight years for me, and I'm enthusiastically heading for another great 38. I plan to be at least 86 before I surrender my gold-plated bowl brush to a younger pro!

For sure, our duties of dislodging dirt have had their moments with us. Who in any profession could tell more guts and glory (and gory) stories than we, the cleaners?

A few years ago, my company was cleaning the big Sun Valley ski resort complex. All kinds of big wheels go there to work and play and attend conventions, and we were the ones who cleaned up after them. In 1971, there was a big national governor's convention there, and plenty of other might-be-president-some-day types were attending too. We worked our butts off to please everyone involved, and it was finally the closing social in the big plush reception room. We had it sparkling and spotless, and when I finished detailing the carpet I ran home to change from my cleaning uniform to my suit for a church meeting later. I returned to the now rapidly filling room where a get-acquainted cocktail party was in full swing. I found my supervisor and we were standing off to the side, reviewing and discussing our after-the-bash cleanup plans.

A large gentleman, dressed to the max and drunk to about the same extent, came swaggering by. His overstacked hors d'oeuvres plate and drink slipped from his hand, all over the expensive, freshly cleaned carpet. He wasn't too far gone to recognize two cleaners, and he pointed his fat finger at us, then at the mess, and loudly yelled, "Hey, clean that up, boy!" In a split second I fell to my knees, whipped out my monogrammed birthday hanky, and efficiently cleaned it up. Then I made a little bow to the man. My supervisor was indignant, if not shocked, and the minute the guy was out of hearing range, said, "That big ill-mannered tub of guts, I wouldn't clean up after him in nine million years!" (Just about everyone's true feelings about people like that.) I led the supervisor even farther out of hearing range and explained to him the most important principle of our business. "Klaus, it's really immaterial whether he's a slob, 100 percent inconsiderate, rude, wrong, or unappreciative. The bottom line is that cleaning up is our job. We're in the service business. We clean, we don't control people's manners. We serve, so let's do it well. Just because he (or fifty more like him) are rude and inept, we don't have to be. We can be superb in our job. What if a dentist looked in our ill-kept mouths and said, 'Why you snacking, candy-eating slob, look at all those rotten teeth. I wouldn't clean and fix them up in nine million years!' Their conduct is our customers' problem, cleaning up is ours. We can't and never will run their lives."

My supervisor understood what I was saying. Just because some of the people we clean up for and around are losers, we don't have to be. If we do a class job, we remain classy people. And that's what this book is about: how you can become a real "Number 1" pro cleaner and love it.

I started cleaning professionally like most of you, kind of by accident. I was a hard worker and a college student who needed to eat and pay for books and classes. My first job was bottling pop on an assembly line. When I got my first paycheck I was shocked to see they had held out some of my money. I'd never heard of that before so I raced down to the boss, slapped the check on the counter

and asked "What is this FICA, State, and Fed stuff?" "It's the law," he said. "I have to hold it out for payroll tax!" "Not out of my check," said I and left the job. Back to my dorm room to grumble and murmur to myself. One good thought popped into my head, why not go into my own business? I announced to my two roommates that I was going into the world of business. One of them said, "You ought to clean houses. I hear people get rich doing that." I remembered how messy many people's homes were and how much I liked to be neat. It sounded like music to my ears. Being a farm boy, I was willing to tackle anything (after all, I cleaned up after pigs and cows for seventeen years).

"How do I do it?" I asked another friend. "Oh," said he, "just go down and put an ad in the paper and everyone will call you." So I did it. The ad cost $1.35 (my first business experience) and it said…

(I'd never even made my bed before.) I waited and three days went by and then my first call. A rich lady up on North 15th, "This is Mrs. Van Snoot, do you clean carpet?" In as gruff and confident a voice as I could muster, I answered, "Yes, I do, M'am." I'd never seen a carpet before; on the farm we still had old linoleum floors and an outdoor toilet! I ran downtown and rented a carpet machine, read the little book that came with it and the print on the shampoo bottle and remembered one important thing about cleaning: Mother always used boiling hot water. Well, this lady had a plush wool carpet, about two inches thick. When the job was done, she thought she had a throw rug. That baby shrank four inches away from the wall. I called a carpet stretcher and got it back in place. Man, shrinkage is powerful—it moved the grand piano!

The next job I couldn't remedy that easily. I was using lacquer thinner in a little sewing room with no ventilation and the lady of the house came running out yelling "My bird is dead, my bird is dead!" The fumes did in the poor canary.

On another job I dripped cleaning solution on top of an armoire while washing the ceiling and left white bleached spots on that gleaming expensive finish. I even liquefied some linoleum once using ammonia and stripper trying to get off the old wax. And (the kind of disaster you only dream about) I once tipped over an antique china closet filled with those 19th century blue and white dishes.

I'm sure you could share similar adventures in learning to clean, but I hung in there. I hired one, then two, then three, then ten, then 20, then 100 fellow students and bought some used trucks and equipment. Between school and cleaning I put in 18-hour days, cleaning supermarkets, banks, homes, office buildings, factories, and hotels, cleaning up after fires, floods, bachelors, animals, and even suicides. All of this I did while going to college. It took six years but finally I made it to graduation day. By now I realized that I loved to clean and for sure I knew more about cleaning toilets than I did about dissecting frogs. So to make a long story short, **I stayed in the cleaning business**.

My cleaning company now is one of the major firms in the industry and has employed more than 40,000 cleaners over the years. I began writing books about cleaning a few years ago and have twenty on the market now. I have a large and fast-growing cleaning museum and library, and the unique cleaning events that are a special feature of my company's annual meetings have received nationwide attention.

Cleaning has given me a good, exciting life and a good living. The better you do it, the better it treats you. No job gives more opportunity for new knowledge, friends, exercise, awareness, and the ability to change or affect the quality of others' lives. I've learned seven building trades just in the course of my cleaning and maintenance activities, and we've all learned hundreds of cleaning secrets and inside wisdom from each other. The purpose of this book is to round it all up, yours and mine, and put it at the disposal of any cleaner. This is a reference book just for our profession. It contains all the instructions and explanations of how to do it in such a way that our lives and paychecks and the quality of our work will be something we can be excited about and proud of every single minute.

P.S. Let me share some of the cleaning nicknames I've picked up along the way.

King of the Toilet Ring
Fastest Bowl Brush in the West
Billy Graham of the Pine-Sol Set
Porcelain Preacher
The Pied Piper of Purification
Baron of the Biffy
Captain Commode
Commodian
Dean of Clean
Jet Set Janitor
Professor of the Potty
Titan of the Toilet Bowl
Flush Gordon
Minstrel of the Mop

Guru of the Loo
Duke of the Dustpan
Urinal Colonel
Mr. Mopp
Don Juan of the John
Housecleaner Extraordinaire
Czar of Cleanliness
Crusader for Clean
Squire of the Squeegee
Ajax Evangelist
Sultan of Shine
The Cleaning Man

(and there are at least 50 more!)

There is no such thing as a temporary job.

If you're thinking about getting or keeping your cleaning job "just to get by" until something better comes along, remember, no job is temporary. Whether you do it for five minutes, five hours, or five years it is and will be a part of your life forever. It engraves habits and attitudes into your being, and habits and attitudes aren't temporary, they stay and transfer everywhere with you to bless or curse you forever. Any activity you engage in for any length of time makes or takes character from you, adds or subtracts commitment, ambition, feelings, and growth. You keep **everything** from every job you take. You don't put your life or abilities on hold for a while to work at something until you land that dream job someday. You can't get back any minute of time any job consumes. Every job puts its brand on you, and whether or not you like or love the job, it's part of you forever.

So no matter when or where or what or for how long you take a job, make sure you do it the best you can, with all your heart, might, mind, and strength. Because the bottom line is that it really has nothing to do with the nature of the job or the pay or who you're working for— only with your personal effort to give your best and become your best. The ultimate in life isn't what you do or get, *it's who you become.* No job is temporary, every job is eternal in the sense of effect. So never think of or treat one lightly, because from any job you'll get a pattern, a rhythm, a satisfaction that will never leave you. *All* is the only way to do it, be it for years or minutes.

There is no such thing as a temporary job!

CHAPTER 1

OUR PROFESSION:
The BIGGEST
and the BEST

> **Do you realize how big our profession is? We are the oldest and largest profession in the world, over 9,000,000 of us in this country alone are in cleaning and maintenance making a living.**

This key

Even more exciting and amazing is the fact that almost every happening in society is housed, processed, or originated in a building—those buildings we have so much charge of and influence over. Our work directly affects the daily flow of almost all human interaction all over the world. We don't just clean up and service the facilities and keep them in good condition, we create the very atmosphere millions and millions of people live and work in every day, influencing their attitude toward their jobs and their homes. It's all in our hands. Most of you will affect more lives than your minister or senator.

that we are handed to clean a building isn't just a key to open a door, shine a floor, or put away a buffer. It unlocks some amazing responsibilities and opportunities. When people see that ring of keys dangling from your belt, hip sagging with the load, they may see only the means for getting into places so that we can clean them. You might look at your keys the same way, but I never have. True, they let you into room after room to clean and service, but they let you into much more than that. Most educational classes or college degrees have a hard time matching what your cleaning keys really do for you. Have you ever looked at the whole job, what your profession really is? You do some of the following, most of it, or all of it.

Janitor duties and responsibilities

As the person in charge of sanitation, you directly influence, affect, or control: ✓ safety ✓ security ✓ building morale ✓ energy use ✓ repairs ✓ depreciation prevention ✓ scheduling ✓ supply use ✓ grounds organization ✓ fire prevention ✓ and ✓ lost and found. You play a big part in public relations, plus you're involved in training, organizing, accounting, purchasing, inventorying, and budgeting. (As well as anything else nobody in the building wants to do at any time, for any reason.)

If you really think about it, it's pretty impressive, almost scary. But look at what

all these "jobs" will mean to you if you learn to do them well. They will make you an expert, a superperson—build you up, educate and refine you.

Too many people in jobs that society admires and praises overestimate their station in life, and underestimate ours. Cleaning, if gone into wholeheartedly, is a chance to never get bored, as so many professionals do in their jobs.

If you just lift your head out of the toilet, quit concentrating on the broom for a minute and look around, you'll discover that nowhere in the world can you find a profession with more facets of interest, challenge, and opportunity. They are there, no matter what type or size of place you clean. You may not need a high level of education to enter this business, but there's no limit to where you can go if you're willing to apply personal intelligence and effort once you get in.

Sadly, when many of you were hired, you were told and have probably repeated to yourself every day since then, the famous line:

> "IT'S A DIRTY JOB,
> BUT SOMEBODY'S GOT TO DO IT."

This, folks, is the biggest reason cleaning is thought of as a nasty job. Because people who know little about it have tagged it with a dead-end label. Even our mothers said to us when we were little, "You better behave, you little snot, or you'll have to clean your room." Or the teacher said, "If you students don't study, you'll end up like Mr. Evans, the janitor!" Well today, like you, I am the janitor out in the hall, and I know I've got a better deal than anyone I work for.

THIS IS YOUR PROFESSION

You either

- ❐ Chose it
- ❐ Were pushed or transferred into it
- ❐ Or took it "until something better comes along."

No matter which of these is you, right now you're a member of the oldest and largest profession in the world. You're being paid to clean and maintain facilities and furnishings and make people happy.

There's no such thing as a temporary job

(Read this one more time now!)

If you're thinking about getting or keeping a job "just to get by" until something better comes along, remember, no job is temporary. Whether you do it for five minutes, five hours, or five years, it takes and uses up your time. It is part of your life forever. It engraves habits and attitudes into your being, and habits and attitudes aren't temporary, they stay and transfer everywhere with you to bless or curse your life forever. Any activity you engage in, short or long, makes or takes character, adds or subtracts commitment, ambition, growth, and feelings. You keep

everything from every job you do. You don't put your life or abilities on hold for a while to work at something until you land that dream job someday. You can't get back even one minute of time a job consumes. Every job puts its brand on you, and whether or not you love the job, it's part of you **FOREVER.**

So no matter when or where or what or for how long you take a job, make sure you do it the best you can, with all your heart, might, mind, and strength. *All* is the only way to do it. Because the bottom line is that it really has nothing to do with the nature of the job or the pay or who you're working for—only with your personal effort to give your best, to become your best. The ultimate in life isn't what you do or get, it's what you become. No job is temporary—and that includes cleaning—(too often labeled temporary); every job is eternal in the sense of effect. So never think of or treat one lightly, because from any job you'll get a pattern, a rhythm, an estimation of yourself that will never leave you.

Not a last chance job!

Ever notice that when someone is out of work, has failed to get a job on several different tries, pretty soon friends and family are jumping in and helping them find "something." Inevitably someone will always say, "Well, have you tried to get a janitor job? It's better than starving." The stigma traditionally attached to cleaning too often projects it as a last resort kind of job, lower than a garbage person or sewage pumper. We hear this so much that many of us cleaners get to believing that we are indeed doing a menial task or have picked a less than first choice profession. BUT knowing more about it, in fact taking a good hard look into the profession, will change your view of it.

Consider the following aspects of the cleaning profession, and compare them with many other jobs. I think you'll come to see that filing reports in a nice office building, in nice clothes, can be more "menial" than cleaning.

Pay

Starting pay is only a foundation. If you check out a few facilities, you'll see that in time the faithful, productive cleaning people are working more steady and earning equal or above average incomes. Most cleaners make more than the secretaries, musicians, schoolteachers, drivers, kitchen workers, parking lot attendants, and clerks who comprise the majority of the work force. Cleaning has its per-capita share of millionaires, too. You might be surprised if you compare yourself around the community. That's why so many people have applications in for cleaning jobs like yours.

Hours

While "janitor hours" may be less desirable for some, others appreciate the quiet and opportunity to work without a crowd around, or constant surveillance. Not having to work at the same time as everyone else is wonderful, when you think about it. This also means that you have time off when everyone else is working, while the roads and recreation facilities are less crowded.

Janitors assigned specific hours can usually modify this schedule in case of emergency or by prior arrangement as long as the work is completed before the start of regular business hours. And there are all kinds of part-time as well as full-time jobs and positions. There aren't many jobs with this kind of flexibility. Cleaning doesn't tie you down, it turns you loose!

Education

The opportunities you get in a cleaning job to learn not only valuable skills but all kinds of things about people and places can't be matched. You see, hear, feel, and smell everything!

Exercise

Plenty of it! People these days are paying for all kinds of potions, pills, classes, and machines to get exercise to keep trim and physi-

cally fit. Our job has built-in bodybuilding benefits. In cleaning you get all kinds of basic exercise—walking, bending, light lifting, climbing, and reaching, etc.—right on the job, so you get paid for it! Cleaning is one of the best personal fitness programs going.

Atmosphere

Almost every job involves pressure—in fact many jobs today have constant, unrelenting pressure that keeps your nerves raw. Not so with a janitor job. A janitor works unhassled, where it is relatively quiet. And you can almost rest emotionally while you work. Cleaning has plenty of responsibilities and duties, but in a relaxed atmosphere and setting. And if done right and well, it will only improve your temperament and add years to your life. This is, or should be, a big factor in choosing a job.

Opportunities for personal growth

Cleaning service is by no means mindless work; it requires good organization and has a great variety of responsibilities for the area in care. "Doing the same old thing" all the time is more of a problem for accountants and secretaries. The opportunity to observe various types of business operations and procedures, and all kinds of people at their best and worst, gives us a wealth of experience and information. You'll find maintenance people better informed than the average worker.

Opportunities for advancement

Looking for a place to go if you are good or when you retire? See p. 101 for a world of possibilities.

In the cleaning field, geography makes little difference. Opportunity is everywhere because dirt is everywhere, in small towns and big cities, hot and cold climates, rural as well as urban areas. The carpet isn't any cleaner on the other side of the state or the other side of the world.

Cleaning, the great launching job!

I cleaned the first building the Bell System ever *contracted* to be cleaned, and later became their single biggest "janitor" doing hundreds of buildings. I even wrote maintenance practices and procedures for them in New York. I was really treated well by their big executives and top managers, and especially by five of their division presidents and vice presidents. One day as I was enthusiastically sharing some new cleaning information with them, one of them said to me, "Did you know that ALL FIVE OF US BEGAN WORKING FOR THE BELL SYSTEM (then the largest company in the world) AS JANITORS?" It was easy to believe. Cleaning launched them on their way to becoming, if not made them into, great men and women. So remember, when you're cleaning anywhere, you are building a launching pad for not just your job but your life. So do it willingly… and well.

There are no dead-end jobs, only dead-end people. The surface of the potential of the cleaning profession hasn't even been scratched yet. This industry is begging for new inventions, products, methods, and skills. KNOWLEDGE and EXPERIENCE in this field are two of the best guarantees for personal security and continued employment. There are millions of workers in other fields with almost no hands-on skills or measurable productivity. Our hands-on business needs hands-on experience, and once you get it, there's no limit to what you can do. Cleaning gives you dozens of job skills that will benefit you and your family.

Chance to make a difference

Isn't it nice to do something—and especially make a living at it—that enhances the quality of others' lives? Your work, which gives places much of their atmosphere and dignity, influences others every hour of the day and lifts their lives and feelings. Not too many jobs do that.

Today, on every job, the big word is "bennies." Translated that means benefits—and when people say that they mean retirement, 401k plans, health insurance, holidays, sick leave, vacation, personal leave, etc. To me these aren't benefits, they're extra, additional forms of compensation and payment for services rendered. Benefits to me are something deeper and much more rewarding than cash accumulation (money has never been a real motivator or happiness maker, and you'll never have enough cash no matter how much you make.)

True benefits are personal things you take with you from a job, what you become from it, not what you get. Getting paid is what just about everyone gets, but getting better as a person is the bottom line for living a happy and productive life. Cleaning seems to produce people who are kind and considerate, and good citizens, not greedy. Overall, cleaning people are sharers, polite and gentle; they have virtues many other professionals seem to lack. These are the gains from cleaning that I look at as _REAL_ benefits.

The Benefits of Your Profession

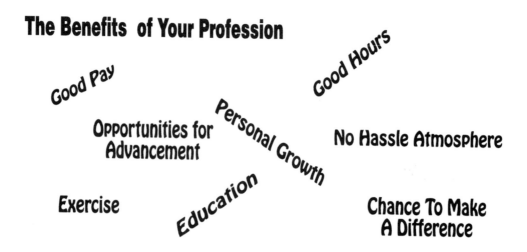

Good Pay

Good Hours

Opportunities for Advancement

Personal Growth

No Hassle Atmosphere

Exercise

Education

Chance To Make A Difference

CHAPTER 2

BEFORE YOU START TO CLEAN: Some Important Things to Be Aware of

What is your job?

To clean? Nope, it isn't that simple. I've found that 95 percent of us cleaning for a living don't know the full truth of what our job is, what we are working at or working for. And this is the reason many people clean well, or even fast and well, but are still failures as professional cleaners. Cleaning is part of your job, true, but there are two other parts even bigger, and there's no way you can ignore them.

We have 3 BASIC OBJECTIVES:

- Keeping the building clean
- Doing it economically (fast)
- Keeping the occupants happy

No single one of these, or combination of only two, will work. They're all equally important and you have to do all three.

7

Your job is to do all three well. So you need to know:

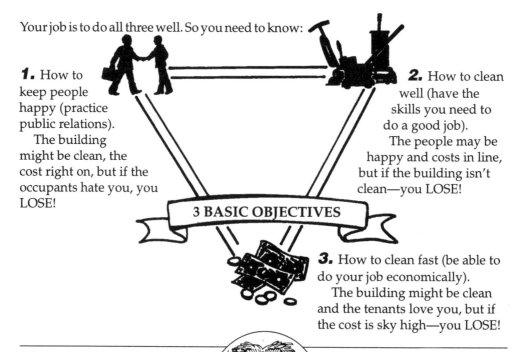

1. How to keep people happy (practice public relations).

The building might be clean, the cost right on, but if the occupants hate you, you LOSE!

2. How to clean well (have the skills you need to do a good job).

The people may be happy and costs in line, but if the building isn't clean—you LOSE!

3 BASIC OBJECTIVES

3. How to clean fast (be able to do your job economically).

The building might be clean and the tenants love you, but if the cost is sky high—you LOSE!

"Janitor" a name to be proud of

After more than 38 years in the business, and even now that I'm an internationally known TV star, best-selling author, corporate chairman and all that, I still introduce myself as Don Aslett, the Janitor. I'm proud of my title and it's an honorable one… from Janus of long ago.

Janus was the Roman god of entrances and exits, of sunrise and sunset. He's usually depicted as having two faces, one looking forward and one back.

In every home, the first morning prayers were addressed to him. Prayers were also said to Janus at the beginning of any important undertaking, such as a war or political campaign.

His aid was sought not only for national problems but also for personal and household undertakings. As the god of beginnings he was also the god of the new

year. From him, we get the word January. He was the god who ruled over progress and civilization. From all of this you can see why he was the ideal god for the custodians of Roman homes and estates to adopt as their special deity. And it's from him that we get the word "janitor."

Many people really get bent out of shape when someone calls them "janitor." They grumble and put out a request to the personnel department or the union that they must be called sanitation engineer, custodian, or some other "decent, respectable" title. But janitor is so simple and classy; it tells people what we do without faking.

In any case, it's the person wearing it, not the job or title itself, that determines the success of any venture. Your own conduct, ability, and enthusiasm for the work you do can make any title a winner.

A young fellow by the name of Mike

Turner, for example, worked for me at a tough cleaning job—others had griped, moaned, and complained as they did it, but not Mike. The more dirt and obstacles were thrown at him, the better he got. He was a real first class man, a top janitor. Then he moved to Boise and continued working for my company. I didn't see him for a year; then I received an invitation to his wedding. You know weddings, everyone dressed up to the max, and in the mingling after the ceremony I asked Mike how things were going, and if he still liked being a janitor. He pulled back his lapels Superman style revealing his company manager identification on one side and my cleaning company logo on the other of his tuxedo shirt. Now that's class!

"How Do I Look?"

No way out of it for a pro cleaner… we have to look good! We have to have our own house in order before attempting to clean up others'.

Neat, clean personal dress and grooming **isn't an option** for a real professional cleaner, nor does it matter whether you're straightening up an elite office or shoveling away the tailings at the Jim Bridger coal mine. We always should have a neat clean appearance. There are too many of us cleaners whose underarm odors outdo the restroom urinal, much to the disgust of those we clean around. As one custodian I complimented for looking good put it, "Well, even an old barn looks better with a little paint." And she did look good, all the time!

It just takes a tiny bit of effort. Let's not have to be told to bathe, shave, trim our hair or moustache, wear fresh clothes, and cover our chimichanga or taco salad breath when we happen to lunch that way.

The clothing doesn't have to be new or expensive, and we don't have to look trendy or stylish, just clean and fresh. That's our whole thrust, our whole life, how we make our livings as professionals, clean and fresh. If we look like a low-life, people will treat us like one. And who will believe we can clean anything if we can't clean ourselves?

Uniforms

The Super Bowl has what they call the million-dollar minute of advertising time. Each sponsor, Ford or Chevy or Bud Light, pays $500,000 for 30 seconds. Just imagine at the next Super Bowl all the players running out on the field in tee shirts and mismatched sweats, with the referees in swim trunks or rumpled pajamas. How much would a minute of advertising be worth then? They'd be lucky to get a sponsor.

Why? It's the same game!

Same players!

Same quality of sport!

Do uniforms make a difference? You bet they do! Let's say you're heading home tonight and suddenly a siren goes off behind you. You pull over and get that sick feeling inside as you see the flashing lights and hear the crunch of gravel. The state trooper strides up to your window and his big booming authoritative voice says "Driving kind of fast, aren't you,

chum?" Your answer is frozen in your throat, you turn your head and there in beach pants, Mickey Mouse hat, and tennis shoes stands the patrolman. What is your reaction? Not fear any more, for sure. You want to laugh. He's still an officer with full authority to arrest and ticket you, but does a uniform make a difference? Unbelievable!

When I first started my cleaning company we (me and all the college students working for me) showed up to work in clean Levi's and nice knit shirts, etc. We were well behaved on the job, didn't smoke, or leer, or cuss. Yet the people of the house or hotel we cleaned always stayed around and kept a close eye on us. One day attempting to be sharper, we found some cheap navy whites (pants and shirts) and put our Varsity logo on the back. From then on it was amazing—people would toss us their keys when we walked in the door and tell us to help ourselves to the fridge and lock up when we left, as they went off about their business. Magic? Nope, just a simple, inexpensive uniform.

I know some of us resent regimentation, in fact probably all of us. But uniforms aren't regimentation, they're our "team jerseys," and not just easier to work in, but a comfort to our clients. Many people are terrified to see a stranger turn up when they're working late in a big building. Or when they see someone knock on the door of an empty house, then watch them haul things in and out. If we're in clearly marked uniforms, on the other hand, people relax and even help. Uniforms give us identity and a place to spread our name, so when someone wants to single us out or get in touch with us, they'll know who to call.

Whether or not a uniform is required where you work, let me assure you, men and women, that a uniform can do more to make you a gentleman or lady of the cleaning realm than almost anything else going. Ball teams play better with uniforms and we clean better, period. I do volunteer work in my off time, cleaning floors or rugs, doing painting for neighbors, a needy person, or family. **Even if I'm working alone, I wear my full uniform,** either whites or a labeled jumpsuit, and boy is it an advantage. Just like when I'm cleaning on a paying job with a uniform, I get respect and cooperation and help I probably wouldn't get otherwise.

Even if a uniform isn't required, get your own and wear it—watch how everything improves.

Some choices here:
**1. Whatever you wear, make sure that it's clothes and shoes you can move, climb, and carry things comfortably in.
2. Regular clothes with hospital-type smocks over them are great for short shift jobs. If the company won't put on the name and emblem, then do it yourself. They'll soon catch the vision.
3. Thrift stores. For a few dollars you can find whites and khakis or blues that match and look "uniformy." Some cities even have uniform outlets, where you can get surplus, obsolete, or "seconds" uniforms inexpensively.
4. Jumpsuits are getting sharper all the time. They come in lots of colors and styles and they're easy to move in and always look good. You don't have to worry about tops and bottoms staying together, or cleaning debris dropping on your bare skin.
5. Tee shirts are low on my list. Collared ones are great but plain tee shirts look good on only on a few of us. And hairy bellies poking out from under any shirt will really put off the public!**

Here's a grooming checklist.

How Do You

✓ Check Out
in Your Job?

Check off the boxes that apply to you.

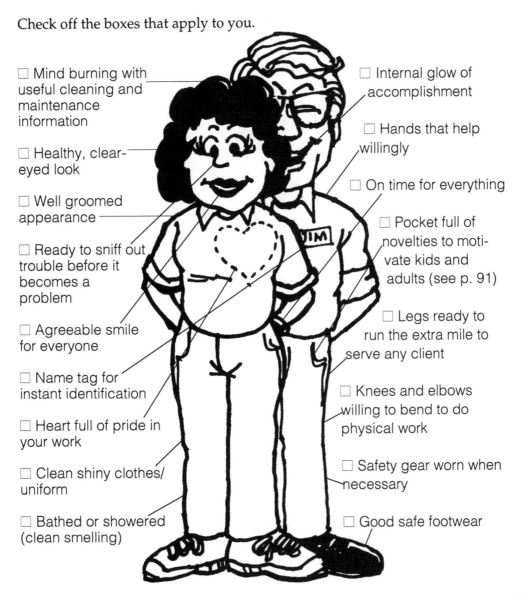

☐ Mind burning with useful cleaning and maintenance information

☐ Healthy, clear-eyed look

☐ Well groomed appearance

☐ Ready to sniff out trouble before it becomes a problem

☐ Agreeable smile for everyone

☐ Name tag for instant identification

☐ Heart full of pride in your work

☐ Clean shiny clothes/uniform

☐ Bathed or showered (clean smelling)

☐ Internal glow of accomplishment

☐ Hands that help willingly

☐ On time for everything

☐ Pocket full of novelties to motivate kids and adults (see p. 91)

☐ Legs ready to run the extra mile to serve any client

☐ Knees and elbows willing to bend to do physical work

☐ Safety gear worn when necessary

☐ Good safe footwear

SAFETY

Living to tell about it, or Our professional obligation to be safe and secure

Don't you like yourself the way you are, with no missing or damaged parts? That's why **safety measures aren't sissy.**

1. Woman died in an elevator when she was caught between the wall and the elevator when it dropped down the shaft.

2. Man killed when he fell from the 25th story because his safety harness broke.

3. An employee working on a project for the company meeting slipped while he was operating a chain saw and nearly amputated two of his fingers.

4. A large metal chalkboard a woman was cleaning fell from the wall and hit her on the head. It caused mental and neurological problems for the rest of her life.

5. An employee lifting a pallet herniated a disk in his back and it caused partial paralysis.

6. A cleaner leaving a building was attacked by a gang of youths with baseball bats. She was badly beaten and her purse and car were stolen.

7. A manager going to bid an account on New Year's Day had his family with him when they were hit at an intersection by another automobile, causing severe injuries to his wife and two small children. Over $200,000 in medical bills alone.

8. An employee attending a company picnic was hit in the head playing baseball, causing severe neurological damage.

9. A top janitor with 15 years' experience reaching into a wastebasket was lanced by a contaminated discarded needle.

10. A janitor noticed the plug on the floor machine was frayed, but he used it anyway and was electrocuted stripping a floor.

These aren't made up, folks, I copied them directly off our Worker's Comp list this morning. Things like this happen all the time to good professional cleaners who consider themselves careful. Any accident can sure ruin your day if not your entire life.

In maintenance, our exposure to safety hazards is much greater than that of most other personnel. Few other professions have the safety risk exposure we do.

Besides the driving, lifting, climbing, carrying, and tool using that other workers do, we must also:

- Work on wet, slippery floors

- Work with dangerous cleaning chemicals

- Work with large, heavy, electrical equipment

- Work on ladders with glass, lights, and windows

- Work during the dark hours of the day

- Do a lot of carrying on stairs

Have you ever stopped to think that in a year at work you might handle at least 100,000 objects, lift over 50 tons of material and furniture, walk, run, or climb over 10,000 miles, climb 62 miles of stairs, smell 300 different chemical odors, etc.?

It can all be exciting and profitable if done safely. If not, it can make a professional cleaning job one of the most miserable experiences of your life (if you manage to live that long).

How I ever got through my first 20 years of cleaning without getting killed or killing someone else, I'll never know. For years, I have to admit that safety and security were just signs for someone else. Like most of you I followed the basic rules for driving, climbing, and bending safely, and obeyed door codes, but I never really pursued the subject much beyond that. It always seemed to happen to the other guy. My paint didn't explode, my people didn't lose keys, I had insurance on my cars, what else mattered? Nothing, until the day we accidentally let a terrorist decoy into a telephone building; one of our window washers, scaffold and all, plunged 14 stories to his death; several of our vehicles were stolen and crashed; two

of our janitors beaten and robbed; and a floor scrubber trailer came loose on Main Street in Salt Lake City and speared a Nova (no one in it at the time, fortunately). These incidents grabbed my attention, and now safety is my *number one* concern in cleaning.

Safety and security isn't a group or gang thing, or something that if everyone else does, then you might follow along. It's a very personal and individual concern—yours. No one should have to serve papers on you or send you to school or pound safety procedures into your skull. Going after all the safety information, skills, and techniques you can, is not just your job, but your own personal responsibility.

"They" aren't going to take care of you and me every day in every way. *We* need to keep our eyes open for safety and security risks, because they're a big danger to us personally. When something gets us, the company may have to pay now but it's OUR mind, body, and limbs that pay the real price over time. If we just head this off, practice careful precautions, we'll have smooth sailing and a positive chain reaction.

13

Almost every company of any size has (or should have) well established safety policies for any situation. So first, **find** and **read** and learn them. It will enhance your job tremendously and save lives, especially the big one—YOURS.

Here are some basics to be aware of in any case, especially if you work for a small company or are self-employed and no one has drilled you.

Some safety policies and basic cautions every cleaner should know

1. Use ladders and scaffolding properly (see p. 18).

2. Wear rubber-soled shoes to help prevent slips and falls.

3. Always put up warning signs—cones, ropes, etc.—before you start working overhead, or applying water or floor finish to a floor. I know inconvenience can quash our common sense, but walk the extra distance and get the barrier.

Barricades are as important as a stop sign at an intersection—they prevent collisions, falls, paint splatters, and ruined clothes and bodies in all kinds of situations. Any time you work in a traffic area with anything that can be harmful, set up the appropriate warning or barricade. This can be a sign or a roped-off area—it takes only a minute and will save major and minor accidents as well as the quality of your "just waxed" floors. Remember, falling on wet floors is the number one accident in our industry. Your balance might be great, but a child's or a senior citizen's isn't necessarily the same.

4. Avoid lifting that twists your body. Lift with your legs, and don't put undue strain on your back. If you're in doubt about how to lift, ask your supervisor. Don't try to lift heavy loads by yourself—get help. Next to falls, lifting injuries are the most common.

5. Always give your job your full attention—don't daydream, engage in horseplay, or isolate yourself with headphones.

6. Be certain that electrical equipment is properly grounded and functioning properly—don't use equipment with frayed cords or missing ground prongs. Don't tape damaged electric cords; replace them.

7. Don't attempt to service equipment without unplugging it first. And unless you've been specifically instructed otherwise, repairs should be performed by your supervisor or a trained technician.

8. Make sure that moving parts (belts, fans, wheels) come to a complete stop before removing covers.

9. Sweep it up, don't pick it up! Sweeping saves time and prevents cuts and puncture wounds.

10. Use proper safety equipment when working with caustic or potentially dangerous tools and chemicals. Just because you are informed or more intelligent than the others in the building doesn't excuse you from goggles, gloves, aprons, or other protective items when they're called for. If the company issues them or they're available, use them.

11. Know the location of emergency equipment in your work area (fire extinguisher, first aid kit, etc.).

12. Be alert to potential safety hazards and report them to your supervisor. In the event of an emergency, first call the proper agency (fire, ambulance, police); then notify your supervisor or manager.

13. Keep treated dust mops away from furnaces, light bulbs, and other heat sources. Dust mops shouldn't be stored sitting flat on the floor but should be covered with a plastic bag and clipped on the wall.

14. Clean equipment after each use. Dirty equipment is unsafe, inefficient, and unprofessional.

15. Don't leave trash in your closet. It's a fire hazard as well as a safety hazard.

16. Obey all company rules and government regulations, all safety signs, markings and instructions that apply to you and your job.

If you are injured at work, no matter how slight the injury, report it to your supervisor immediately.

GLOVES
GOGGLES
GOOD AIR—
THINK!

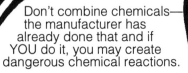

Don't combine chemicals—
the manufacturer has
already done that and if
YOU do it, you may create
dangerous chemical reactions.

Add the chemicals to the water, not
the water to the chemicals. There'll
be less chance of a dangerous splash.

NEVER switch containers or put cleaning
chemicals in an unmarked container, and
especially never store them that way.

Make sure all your spray bottles are clearly labeled
per OSHA requirements.

If you don't know what's in a bottle or container (it
isn't labeled), then get rid of it, or it will linger on to
kill or hurt someone or a surface.

DON'T give your friend or neighbor the "better,
stronger" stuff for home use. Professional chemicals
call for professional training and pro safety precautions.

Don't try to salvage ancient or tiny amounts of leftover
chemicals. It's not worth it.

Avoid the use of BLEACH whenever you can. It's an
imposter. It may whiten things (remove the color from
them), but it doesn't necessarily remove the problem,
and it's really hard on many of the things we use it on.

Store the bad stuff out of everyone's reach—that
means LOCKED away.

Learn your city or county rules for disposal of
hazardous waste (many cleaning chemicals are
indeed that). Then not only observe them but
BE THEIR CHAMPION.

Keeping healthy while cleaning

New days have brought new diseases, like AIDS, and anyone who cleans will have some exposure to the causes (discarded or hidden drug apparatus, blood-borne pathogens, etc.). Following all the new preventatives and cautions, and the new laws is smart. So be smart, and if someone doesn't show you or require you to learn them, do so on your own, because YOU are the main beneficiary.

Where there is odor, there are germs. And you want to protect yourself against disease germs of all kinds.

Ways you can pick up communicable diseases:

- from door knobs and handles

- from discarded food

- picking up used tissues and paper towels

- picking up toilet paper from around toilets. People don't always get it in the toilet after wiping, or might use it to mop up urine after an accident and then leave it on the floor.

- from body wastes of any kind

- while handling garbage bags from bathrooms

Wear rubber gloves while:

- cleaning and disinfecting toilets and urinals

- mopping and disinfecting the soiled area around toilets, tubs, showers

- picking up any dampened or previously dampened towels or washcloths made of cloth or paper, used for personal hygiene

- picking up tissues or hankies used for blowing nose, wiping mouth or eyes

- handling paper towels, rags, or anything used to clean up after a bloody accident (bloody nose, menstrual flow, blood from cuts or wounds)

- wiping up or handling anything used to clean up **any** kind of body discharge

ALWAYS protect yourself with rubber gloves when doing jobs like these. The little cracks from chapped hands or cuts can be enough to expose you to the AIDS virus or other dangerous diseases.

When it's not possible for some reason to wear gloves for such jobs, always wash your hands and wrists thoroughly afterward with soap and water, before you do anything else. This will prevent germs from being passed from your hands to your own face, mouth, nose, and eyes. And help prevent the spread of germs from one area to another.

You don't want to infect anyone else with your own ailments either, so wash your hands well too after using the bathroom, blowing your nose, or sneezing. Keep yourself healthy while cleaning. If you have any doubts or fears about health risks, check with your boss or supervisor immediately.

Getting to the top...
and
STAYING SAFE

Walls

Trees

Lights

Windows

Ceiling Vents

High Decorations

Treed cats

...and 100 more too
scary to mention.

I'm so terrified of high places, whenever I go over the side for high windows I leave fingernail claw marks halfway down the building. But whether or not we fear (or respect) heights, we are in a profession that requires reaching high places. Climbing the wrong way or on the wrong stuff can result in FALLING. People really get bent when you fall on them, and if you kill yourself in the process, you ruin things for your boss as well as your friends, family, and yourself!

So right now, QUIT all of the following and don't do them any more (I know we all have climbed on things like these)

Chairs
Compound any awkwardness at least eight times. So sit on them—never stand.

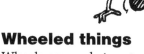

Wheeled things
Wheels are made to roll... and they will!

Mantels
And other ledges and trim are made for looks, not load-bearing strength. It doesn't take much to make them shear right off—with you still on them.

Fixtures
Were made to wash hands, not wipe out lives. Don't stand on them; they aren't made to take it.

If...

✔ **You are afraid of heights,** don't push yourself. Tenseness has a tendency to make us accident prone.

✔ **You can't find a way** to get up there, hire an expert or rent a safe platform or scaffolding. You won't become a hero by overextending yourself.

✔ **You have lots to carry** up a ladder or climb with, make multiple trips or strap stuff to you; don't occupy your hands.

✔ **You leave ladders** or other reaching tools around after a task is over, you invite security violations and thievery, as well as possible accidents.

REACHING TECHNIQUES

Think first: How can I reach it while keeping my feet on the floor?

Because you (not the company) has to do the work, you know the tools you need to do it. And you need to initiate the correct purchases and then take good care of the tools.

Always use ladders and scaffolding correctly and carefully. Don't overreach or take chances. If you haven't been trained in the proper use of ladders or scaffolding or you're in doubt, ask for help! (While you're still standing on the floor, not lying there wounded!)

Before you go up, make sure barricades are in place. Someone else bumping into even a safe setup can cause accidents.

Extension handles come in 4-8, 6-12, 8-16 and longer lengths. All sorts of attachments can be placed on the end to do just about anything a cleaner needs to do, anywhere a cleaner needs to do it.

Scaffolding For working in really high places—nothing beats good scaffolding.

•If you have repeated need to do a particularly high job, it pays to buy scaffolding to fit it.

•Always use the recommended outrigger and rails, no matter how "safe it looks already."

•Climb down to move it. Having someone scoot a scaffold with you along for the ride generally means a quick trip to the hospital.

•Keep all your cleaning stuff on the platform or close to it to avoid extra steps and reaching over.

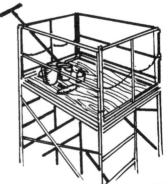

Stepladders Make sure, for your sake and the boss's, that you have the right ladder to fit the job and the building, preferably one you can carry. Stepladders are relatively inexpensive, so having two (one small and one large) is ideal. Heavy duty, commercial grade aluminum or fiberglass is best.

- Stay off the top two steps!

- Make sure the legs are on firm footing and that the hinges **are locked!**

- Empty the platform before you attempt to move a ladder.

- Put your name on your ladders (they walk away!).

- Never paint ladders—it makes them slick and hides weak spots.

Extension Ladders In all my years of frequently using this type of ladder I've never had or seen an accident because I follow the rules:

- Keep it away from anything electrical.

- Make sure the ladder is firmly anchored. If there is no solid, nonslip surface available to set it on, use a rubber pad.

- Make sure your ladder is set at a safe angle. Tilt the bottom out one (1) foot for every four (4) feet of ladder height.

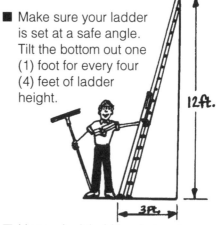

- Hang, don't hold buckets, etc. while you're on it.

- Always keep one hand firmly gripped on the ladder.

- Always pad the top if the surface it contacts is damageable.

Planks Are time savers and surprisingly safe if you use your head and use good quality planks.

- They save you climbing up and down twenty times in a thirty-minute job.

- Reaching across with a plank beats leaning over on a ladder.

- All sorts of variations and combinations of planks can be used on

stairways and landings. With a stepladder, extension ladder, and plank combination you can conquer almost any stairwell quickly and safely.

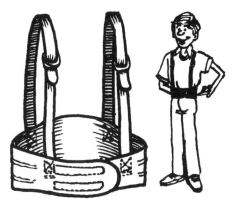

Lifting belts Lifting is the number two enemy of all good cleaners, and it comes with every task. Fortunately most of our stuff is light enough to make for good safe exercise. But the exceptions always pop up, and sometimes they are BIG HEAVY things. Dropping heavy items often damages the surroundings. With no one else around we may go it alone, unprepared, and sooner or later we will pay for it. Yet getting help is so simple, makes so many friends, and so much sense. For those of us who lift often, there are lifting belts available. Ask your boss about them if you need one.

SECURITY (You are in the Secret Service!)

Most of our jobs involve the protection of thousands of people, millions of dollars' worth of equipment, and often restricted information that affects national security. Ours is a unique position when it comes to security exposure, too:

1. We have access to 95 percent of the building, including areas containing restricted equipment, confidential data, or classified information. Most other workers are confined to certain areas. Who has more keys and code access to buildings than we do, when someone wants to break in? It's scary. I once carried the means to get into the entire Bell System's underground (bombproof) communication vaults, a few codes and one key!

2. We often have access to buildings on a 24-hour basis. Other departments normally have only 8-hour shifts.

3. Eighty percent of the service we do is done at night or otherwise during the "off" hours most susceptible to security problems.

4. We are sometimes required to admit outside contractors such as carpet cleaners, painters, plumbers, repairmen, etc., to the building. This greatly increases the likelihood of breaches of security.

5. The high rate of employee turnover in cleaning can accelerate instances of unauthorized or untrained persons seeking admittance.

☛IMPORTANT: All of you will have specific security rules, some more and some less than the general ones I have listed here. Know and follow YOUR company's or client's rules FIRST!

Prevention

1. Know and understand the operating hours and your cleaning time. Then stick to them. Do not enter unauthorized areas, have unauthorized people accompany you into a secure area, or occupy your work area at unauthorized times. Don't go roaming throughout the building unauthorized—stay in your assigned work area.

2. Always wear your uniform while working and have other identification as required.

3. Never report to work while under the influence of alcohol or narcotic drugs, or use these substances during work periods.

4. Don't bring pets, children, friends, or relatives to work with you.

5. Entrance doors to buildings, offices, and suites must be kept locked at all times during off hours, perhaps even during cleaning. Entrance doors must be locked even when you go out only briefly to empty trash or get supplies. And **NEVER** prop them open to prevent them from locking.

Always check windows, doors, and other entrances to your area before leaving to make sure that everything is securely locked.

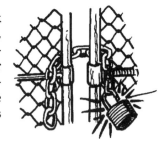

6. Keys are issued only by your supervisor and should **never be duplicated**. Keys issued to you are your personal responsibility and should not be in the possession of any other person. Your keys should be used only to accomplish your assigned work, and loss of them should be reported immediately.

Door entrance codes and combinations should never be divulged to anyone. Codes are used to identify keys and tags, and they should never be marked to plainly indicate what building they unlock. Avoid any kind of written identification on keys. Marked lost keys are a free ticket into the building!

If people are supposed to be in the facility at unusual times, they will have their own keys.

7. Be constantly alert for things that could pose security problems and report them at once. For example:

- Broken windows
- Broken doors
- Damaged locks/door casings
- Fire or safety hazards
- Broken water pipes
- Plugged sewers or other flooding
- Unauthorized people in building
- Bomb threats
- Riot or civil disorder

Stay alert for security threats every hour of your working shift and REPORT ANY POTENTIAL SECURITY BREACH IMMEDIATELY. As well as any violation of company or building security regulations you observe while on the job.

Keeping yourself in the clear

 Don't make personal or other calls from any telephone (other than a pay phone) located in the building(s) where you work, except in the case of emergency.

 NEVER sit at or open any drawers, doors, cabinets, or any container not directly involved in the performance of your work.

 Never loan, give, sell, take, or destroy any equipment, supplies, tools, or personal items encountered in your work.

 Don't use any of the noncleaning equipment in the buildings where you work, including copy machines, typewriters, computers, calculators, etc. And do not turn on or off any equipment that is to be cleaned while carrying out your duties.

 Turn in to your supervisor any money, jewelry, or other items of value you find while working. No pirating trashed junk, shop scraps, etc.

 Never give, sell, or otherwise make available to any person or agency any records or other property of a client, including the contents of wastebaskets.

Always use good judgment when throwing out waste and trash. Many times important records are placed in, on, or near the floor or wastebasket. If there is any question in your mind, ask your supervisor.

Often, when a theft or other security violation occurs in a building, the cleaning crew comes under suspicion. We may be asked to clear ourselves by submitting the entire crew or suspected members to a polygraph examination. Your submission to such an examination, should it ever become necessary, is a condition of employment. Refusal to submit to examination will cast suspicion on you even if none is justified. So smile and cooperate!

Confidential information

You should recognize that certain information you receive as an employee of your company is confidential, and must not be divulged either while you are employed or after separation. Information classed as confidential includes, but is not limited to:

■ Identity of clients

■ Pricing of goods and services

■ Company wage and compensation structure

■ Personnel requirements of various accounts

■ Company methods and procedures

■ Other trade secrets

The divulging of proprietary information may be damaging to a company and could result in your being held liable for such damages.

PROFESSIONAL ETHICS

An overall look at THE BOSS and "THE COMPANY" we work for: They are the reason for our job; they give us the chance to earn a living. They ought to be our best friend, and we theirs!

The process is simple. The boss/company buys (pays for) our time to service his clients or customers. This means serve them—not judge, cuss, or evaluate them, but clean up before and after them. We keep the boss happy by keeping the customers happy.

Because the boss and the company are buying our time, they're pretty sensitive about how we use it on the job. This is just a principle we're all familiar with—wanting to get what you pay for.

We have a true obligation here. It isn't right or honest to take someone's money and then not deliver the time, work, and effort we promised and sold in exchange.

For example, one time I hired a cleaner and paid him $8 an hour. He worked the night shift, alone. At 1 a.m. he slipped into the rear storage room and sacked out (slept) for two hours. Then he got up,

finished his work, and went home. Those two hours cost me $16—he took it, no different than if he reached into my back pocket and took it out of my wallet. If you hire a plumber who spends two hours fixing your pipes, then lies down on your couch for an hour and bills you for three, would you be happy? Your boss works as hard as you do. Do you earn the money he or she pays you?

When you stop work to:

- **make personal phone calls**
- **smoke**
- **take extended breaks**
- **visit**
- **take care of personal business**
- **rest**
- **walk around doing nothing**
- **daydream**

You are stealing—taking money dishonestly. Bosses and companies hate this; they can't afford it. I've seen $12-an-hour cleaners come in 15 minutes late, make four 15-minute phone calls, take two 15-minute breaks, and spend 30 minutes discussing marriage problems, all in the course of one shift. That's 2 1/2 hours, or $30, the boss paid for nothing that day. Companies, schools, churches, and bosses aren't rich; they don't exist just to provide you with a check. They're just like you, when you're shopping for a home or car—they want to get their money's worth!

CHAPTER 3

ON THE JOB: Where You Control "CLEAN"

The doctor arrives in the operating room with scalpel, sponges, and clamps ready for surgery, the performer comes on stage with every prop in place, the ballplayer runs on the field to compete and the field is trimmed and chalked, but we cleaners have no such luxury. The condition we find at work time is either how we left it or how others left it. No one is responsible for setting up our work station for us. We are kind of "lone wolves," basically a one-person show. Let's quickly appraise our domain:

> **As a true professional, remember that from now on it's never "the" janitor closet, it's MY janitor closet!**

Your janitor closet

This little room, whether it's a cleaning cave, an obstacle course of steam pipes, the building junk storage shed, or a sinkless vertical tomb in which to park the Tidy Bowl, is your home base in the building. So making the best of what you have will save a lifetime of Shoulds, What Ifs, I'm Gonnas, and Why Don't Theys. We could each write a book on the personalities of janitor closets we've inherited and fought to find space in. Be that as it may, *this* is our home and always will be as far as the public and the building manager are concerned. It's our launch pad in the morning, our nightly cleanup and storage depot, our message center, and our replenishing center coming and going. It's also thought of as a great place for everyone else in the building to toss litter, clutter, and leftovers.

I remember one night in a large telephone company office someone stuffed all the computer billing cards for the whole month's long distance calls in the janitor closet with no note, nothing. It looked like garbage to me, so I trashed all five boxes. Three days later they came wandering around asking where their billing cards were. Gone! So the whole region had a free month of long distance dialing, compliments of the city landfill.

I've seen some of your closets (and sad to say, some of mine, too) where you could catch a disease just walking by. The buffer in there looked like a dirt clod with a handle on it, and the odor was so bad it was bending the door outward. Some of the stuff stored on the shelves was so old the labels were made before printing was invented. There were 2000 rolls of toilet paper taking up space, all the wrong size for any holder in the building, but they were being kept just in case. Mops stiffer than the Statue of Liberty's hair, old sponges that crumbled like ash when you touched them, a 55-gallon drum of something no one knows what it is or how to

find out. A mop bucket with a flat tire, a 24-quart bucket so full of crud there is now room for only 12 quarts in it, yellowing salespeople's business cards plastered all over the walls—need I go on?

There is one very good reason to avoid this, the thought a sight like this brings to mind:

How can we clean other people's places if we can't keep our own house clean?

This is a justifiable question the public, our company, and bosses will ponder, and the only logical answer doesn't leave us any choice. There is only one solution:

A perfectly neat and clean place to begin and end our day in professional cleaning.

I'm not talking about an annual dig out and restoration party. I mean a continually neat and clean abode for you and all your equipment. A clean closet will bless you, motivate you, organize you, and enhance all your efforts at work and in life.

Don't try to tell me no one notices or sees in there. Everyone sees your closet and forms an opinion. So just put your closet on the same schedule as the building you clean, do it every day (the very end of the day is a good time) and that's it… problem solved.

Here's a checklist for de-cluttering your closet:

■ Arrange all your chemicals and equipment neatly. Put all the cleaners in one area, the cloths all on one shelf or in one bag or box or corner, tools on the right kind of hook or rack. And so on.

■ Clean (rinse, wipe, dust) your equipment and machines at the end of each work period. See p. 32.

■ Make sure all spray bottles are labeled or marked with the contents and OSHA requirements are met. Face all labels outward.

■ Hang mops, dustpans, brooms, and other tools on racks or hooks.

■ Keep large heavy items on lower shelves.

■ Never store even small amounts of trash in the closet.

■ Keep shelves free of paper, clutter, and debris. Janitor closets are not an extra storage area for the entire building.

■ Clean (sweep and mop) the floor of your closet nightly.

■ Clean the sink at the end of your work period.

■ Never leave personal items or treasures in the closet.

■ Turn out the lights and make sure the door is locked when you leave.

■ Have a nice bulletin board for a communications center where you can post notes and schedules as well as legal, safety, and security sheets as required.

■ Keep a little extra door paint in your janitor closet so that you can keep the door touched up. It gets more abuse than any door in the building.

> **It's time we came out *of the closet... CLEAN!***

Ordering and stocking SUPPLIES

It comes as a surprise to most people that only about 5 percent of the cleaning and maintenance budget is for cleaning materials and supplies. Yet the value of supplies to a cleaner is exactly like gas to an automobile—without the right kind and the right amount in the right place at the right time, nothing is going anywhere!

It seems we always have extremes in supplies... either not enough or so much we can't get it all in the closet! The person who provides the supplies and equipment is usually NOT the person using them, so it's easy to end up with too much, not enough, or the wrong kind. This has caused friction in the cleaning world for years. At least 90 percent of cleaning people whimper about their supplies and equipment—it seems to be a constant irritation between the getters and the users—one basing value on price, the other on performance alone.

Here are some guidelines to help make peace and achieve cleaner buildings:

1. The user, the pro cleaner on the front lines, has to communicate with and convince "purchasing" or the owner of what is needed, why, and when. Most owners only hear complaints and problems—seldom direct useful information or solutions.

2. Supplies are not generic. They must fit the building, in both type and amount. I see cases of chrome polish in buildings with no chrome, shelves full of sanitary napkins in buildings with only one or two women, big buffers in the janitor closets of totally carpeted buildings, etc. Equipment, finishes, and cleaners have to fit the building, just as your clothes have to fit you.

3. Get all that old, unused stuff out! Some buildings have ten-year-old materials stored in the closet, paper in sizes that won't fit the dispensers, cleaners no one will use, broken parts of sinks that expired 20 years ago. Because many different people use the closet, everyone thinks someone else owns or wants or is keeping it. This goes on for years, and before you know it, the closet is wall-to-wall clutter. Nothing that isn't in use or doesn't fit the building should be left in the closet. A junkyard closet cools down

the boss from buying anything more, when they look in and see it filled to the brim. The pads may not fit the buffers, but if they are there, you won't get more or better.

4. Keep active, everyday working storage apart from long-term storage. Filters, for example, that you change yearly shouldn't be right in front of the neutral cleaner you use every night. Keep active and inactive material and equipment separate. Keeping scaffolding that you use once or twice a year in your small closet is suicide and cuts the efficiency of the whole building.

5. How much do you want to keep on hand? Most people find that a 3-month supply of inventory is about right.

6. Your vendors, or the places and people you buy supplies from, should be one of your most important allies. Pick and judge the ones you keep by these supply guidelines:
    a) quality of the product
    b) amount of user training, information, and advice available
    c) price
    d) delivery
Good materials may be double the price of the cheap ones and still be less expensive, if you save labor. Labor is 70 percent of maintenance costs, supplies only 5 percent. Good service and dependable deliv-

ery mean you won't have to stockpile too much, so you won't have too much of your space or money tied up. This is a big consideration in choosing and working with a vendor.

> **Salespeople and advertisements on every side will tempt you to overload with supplies, equipment, and materials. Remember, there's no miracle in the bottle. Skilled and intelligent use can cut the supplies needed. At least HALF of normal use is WASTE.**

Your tools of the trade—protect them!

When you stop to think about it, we really have some great gear to eliminate the dirt from places we clean. I'd sure hate to go back to the old broom and sweeping compounds days, when we picked up garbage in a cardboard box and scrubbed and buffed with limp bassine brushes. There are two big problems here in the subject of cleaning tools and equipment, however:

1. We gradually get to a point where we don't appreciate how good we have it; And **2.** Our management and bosses have no comprehension of what we need. Too often they seem to think we ought to do the job with a rag and a bucket or a 37¢ mop head that sheds. We can best change our superior's value system here by being careful to keep what we do have in superb shape.

Example: We get a new Eureka Sanitaire upright vacuum. The company paid $169.95 for it wholesale and it works won-

derfully and we're grateful to get it. It should last a few years (some go 15). Then like all new things, we just use and abuse it till it starts to go downhill. We vacuum up quarters and paper clips, a rubber band or two, even a shoelace. We know we should empty the bag more often, but "tonight is extra busy I'll get it tomorrow for sure." As the newness wears off, we quit rolling up the cord and just drag and bunch it, then go so far as to yank the cord out of the plug from across the room (after all 50 feet is a long way to walk by 11 p.m.!). Our new vacuum is slowly becoming unhealthy from this abuse, getting emphysema of the bag, cancer of the canister, congestion of the beater bar, but as long as it hums when we push the switch, all is well. Six months have gone by, so has our deep appreciation for another "new and nice" thing to clean with. It begins "not to pick up so well" and we have to make two swipes instead of one to get that peanut shell. Gradually our production time slows down and vacuuming now takes twice as long. The plug finally breaks off that vacuum on the busiest, latest night. We stop and wander through the halls looking for a part, tape or something. We wake up the security guard, so together we wander for thirty minutes hunting down a remedy so that vacuuming can go on. Then we find an engineer ($50 an hour) who's working on the HVAC. He's a nice guy, loves to help a janitor in distress, so he drops his tools and now three of us are wandering, broken plug in hand. An hour and a half later the vacuum is fixed and we are back in action. The next night the beater bar (which we have allowed to become impacted with string, rubber bands, and packing tape) has chewed off the belt and frozen up the roller. We stop and dig it free and finish doing half a job because

there's no belt on it now (we don't have a spare). A couple days later the nice bumper guard that protects the furniture, walls and doors, slips while we are hauling the machine around and we never get around to putting back. Now we're in real trouble, the desk legs and doors of all five executive boardrooms are chipped, scratched, and gouged, and the staff is in an uproar. Of course we curse that stupid old, no good vacuum, which unfortunately doesn't have Medicare. So now we put in a requisition for a new model. This one is hashed!

I've seen this happen thousands of times with all kinds of cleaning equipment, and here is the moral of the story: by the time you add up the cost of down time, repairs, lost labor, the complaint factor, and repairs from damage to the facility, this typical six-month to a year-old $169 vacuum costs more like $800!

Think a minute—

A 5-second preventive

(picking up the nail, rolling up the cord, pulling the plug by hand) can prevent:

5 minutes spent trying to dig something out of the vacuum.

5 hours or 5 days waiting for the cord or the ground prong to be repaired.

A $5 replacement part can prevent:

$50-$100 motor fan repair jobs.

$500 worth of labor lost in a year.

$5000 worth of damage to walls, doors, and furnishings, or a personal injury bill!

It seems it's always the other jerks who treat stuff bad, not so! We can help out here by taking conscientious care of all equipment and supplies in our possession.

Forget the notion, "Well, it's the company's, not mine." Wrong again. If it's in **our** custody and control, it may be an asset of the company, but the responsibility for its condition and function is solely ours. Keeping tools operating is an ethical duty we all have, not just a physical one. It's just like when we borrow something, we should treat it better than our own.

Here are the basics of professional care to learn and remember

1. Fix it before it breaks: This means replace parts (belts, bags, mop heads, wheels) when they begin to sag, wobble, fray, crack, or split—don't wait until they break or fall off and the machine stalls.

2. Clean anything you use before putting it away. A clean wipe when the dirt or mucky stripping water on the cord is fresh takes only a second. Leave it for later and it takes hours (if you can chisel it off at all). See p. 33 for details.

3. Empty items regularly before they get full or bulge or overflow. Dirt doesn't have to reach the top to signal dumping time.

4. Put everything away after use… even if you are going to use it again later or tomorrow. If it's left out, it's in the way and all too handy for someone to fall over, borrow, or even steal.

Store things—hang, shelf, or park them—properly. Raise the buffer off the pads, dust mop heads off the floor, etc.

5. Report anything that's down or broken beyond your ability to repair. Don't wait until later or the next time you need it to decide you better get with it and get it patched or replaced. Janitorial equipment doesn't heal itself, you know.

6. Never loan out company tools. Ever notice how outsiders (non-cleaning people) are always eyeing, marveling over, and lusting after our cleaning tools and equipment? Think back for a minute, how many times have they asked you about one of the tools or cleaners you were using?

Never take home, without full official (written if necessary) permission, any of the boss's or company's equipment for personal use. And don't lend or rent to others such as friends, family members, or other company employees. Even if it is "just sitting around there all weekend."

There are only these six basic rules, and if you follow them the long-range spinoffs are so tremendous you won't believe it. You'll solve all kinds of safety problems, security problems, property damage problems, complaint problems, production problems, public appearance problems—it's almost unbelievable what simple maintenance does. And best of all it forms a pattern of habit for you in your everyday personal life, to help you live and work more smoothly and efficiently.

The key to equipment economy is not in the equipment as it appears, it's in the labor, our labor. What speeds us up or slows us down is critical. Which is why proper care of our tools makes all the difference.

TOOL TLC

How many times have you heard the comment that the mechanic's rags, coveralls, and tools were dirtier than the motor? If a doctor or dentist went to work on you in a bloodstained smock or the restaurant served you on dirty dishes or a soiled tablecloth, you'd be aghast, maybe

sick to your stomach. Well that's how we look to others with dirty, damaged cleaning equipment.

Likewise, when we carry around or clean with items that are shabby, we look shabby, we do shabby work, we feel shabby and the bottom line is, we *are* shabby. There is absolutely no excuse for not keeping our equipment clean and in good working order. It takes only minutes and saves hours (as well as our image and maybe even our job). We're judged by how our equipment looks and functions almost as much as by the actual work we do.

Professionals treat the equipment assigned to them as if they had purchased it themselves. They keep it looking good and safe to use, and they make it last.

Buckets, pails, and wringers Rinse at the end of each shift. Use the right size for the job; make sure that all bolts and screws are secure or replaced immediately if missing. Keep casters clean and lubricated; replace them when defective.

Wet mops Rinse thoroughly and wring out before storing. Drape over the wringer to air dry, hang on clamps over the mop sink, or store on a wall hanger that allows air circulation. Label mops, for example, SCRUB, RINSE, FINISH, and never interchange their use. New mops should be soaked in clean water for about 4 hours before using. Don't bleach mops!

Cleaning cloths Make sure used, dirty cleaning cloths are removed from the closet weekly for cleaning.

Dust cloths Dispose disposables, wash the washables, and reuse the live ones.

Brooms Never store them with their bristles or fibers resting on the floor—use broom holders. Keep the bristles free of dirt and debris by brushing them clean. Never use a broom as a squeegee to push water. Alternate the handle on both sides of a push broom to wear and bend the bristles evenly.

Dust mops Vacuum or comb at the end of each shift and cover the head with a plastic bag to prevent oil stains in the janitor closet. Never use dust mops on wet or oil soaked floors. Always store in a well-ventilated closet or locker with the mops hanging free of each other, the wall, and the floor. Follow manufacturer's directions for cleaning and treating.

Dust pans and counter or foxtail brushes Hang at the end of the shift.

Lambswool or feather dusters Can be washed like human hair if they become grimy and matted. Lather with a bit of shampoo, rinse well, comb, and spin briskly between the palms of your hands to fluff out the head. Then hang up the duster to dry.

Vacuums and cords Clean (and check vacuum bags) weekly. Turn the pile selector on vacuums to the correct setting for storage.

Buffers Clean the entire machine and the cord after each use. Use grounded adapter plugs if cord is not equipped with a grounded plug. Repair frayed or cut cords immediately. Wear nonskid footwear whenever you're working on a wet floor. Have a qualified person make all necessary repairs. Operate the machine with care; avoid tangling the cord in the brush.

Floor machine pads and brushes

Never carry floor machine brushes on the handles of the machine. Don't store buffers on their drive brushes and pads. Always store brushes on a wall hangers or lay them on their wooden backs. Keep the bristles clean of dirt and abrasive debris like filings. Try to keep wood backs as dry as possible. Check the locking arrangement for loose or missing screws. Never place brush under machine and lock into place by running motor; always secure brush by hand.

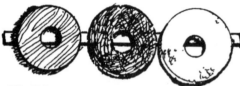

Wet/dry vacuums Always be sure to follow the manufacturer's instructions for use. Check cords for and make any needed repairs before using the unit. Make sure the cord is properly grounded. Wear nonskid footwear when using on a wet operation. Thoroughly clean the vacuum inside and out at the end of each shift. Check the overflow mechanism and keep it clean so that it operates properly. Repairs should be made by qualified personnel.

Brute or cart
Wash out every two weeks.

A good cleaner is energy and environment conscious

Few people on this earth are in a better position to help preserve and restore our planet than you, the cleaner. Here's a real chance to be not just a professional but a good neighbor and good citizen—in fact, a custodian of the universe. Huge buildings, areas, and grounds are in your hands, all the controls that start and stop and run and maintain them. One janitor makes thousands of dollars of difference a year when it comes to energy and the environment—we can do a great deal to prevent and reduce damage, cut costs, and improve quality.

Power My company once came up with an approach for a big Western Electric plant of cleaning one floor at a time with a gang, rather than the way they always did it before, with eight people working away separately on eight different floors for a full eight hours. This single janitorial idea earned a $10,000 energy saving award. Exercising lighting controls, working out stripping schedules that will save hot water, not heating up the whole building to clean for fifteen minutes, etc., not only saves our clients money, it helps prevent waste of the energy sources we all need for the future.

Water Who uses and controls more water than you do, cleaning, flushing toilets, sprinkling lawns, watering plants, hosing down walks, and doing windows? You have the chance to waste or conserve, and the choice you make here will hurt or help your company and the planet immensely. Watching for and preventing drips, adjusting sprinklers, drinking fountains, toilets, etc., adds up over a year's time to a tremendous savings of a precious resource.

Chemicals

 Who deals in more chemicals than we do? Very few, I assure you. We handle and use them all, from alkalis to acids, solvents to paints, disinfectants to pesticides, liquids and powders and pastes and distillates and all their relatives. We are the ones who choose when and where and how much is used, and how things are stored and disposed of afterward. It is scary, and it should inspire and motivate us to read and follow label directions carefully and learn and practice only the right procedures.

Furnishings

 Premature or unnecessary wear and premature discarding of non-working things is a big part of our national waste of resources and energy. How we clean and fix and repair and care for any furnishing can increase or decrease its life up to 500%. A properly cleaned carpet can last fifteen years; a poorly cleaned and cared for one only 3 to 5 years. We could cut trash disposal and manufacturing needs in half just by better cleaning.

Trash and waste

 No one will argue with or challenge us on this one—man, we get it all, every form and type. The public tosses it (in and out of containers), and we gather it, haul it, and heave it. Containing the trash properly is important, because it's the number one litter source in the world. And recycling it whenever we can is the number one solution to saving the planet.

Landscaping

 or plant life. There is almost as much vegetation inside the buildings we clean now, as on the outside. It requires moisture, fertilizer, pruning, and other care not previously a part of the cleaning operation. The way we maintain the landscaping, inside and out, directly affects the universe and all of our natural resources. Another reason to practice good environment-minded maintenance skills.

Pollution

 might be blamed on the big factories and 115 million cars and some wood stoves, but remember, our buildings—little "factories" in their own right— have plenty of cars and trucks coming and going, as well as incinerators and balers and exhausts of all kinds, much of it coming from cleaning and care of the place. We are big time into this universal problem right now. Working on it day to day as we do, we are in a good position to teach and preach and help others get involved. (After our own controls are in effect, of course!)

WELL, ARE WE AN IMPORTANT COG IN THE WHEEL OF CONSERVATION, OR NOT?

A few specifics now:

- Make sure furnaces, pilot lights, gas jets, and filters are checked and cleaned regularly to make sure everything in the building is using energy efficiently. This will also help ensure the longest possible life for the equipment.

- Conserve energy by leaving the heat off or on the night setting without turning it up. All we have to do is dress warmly, keeping in mind that we can always take off a layer of clothing if we get too warm. Heating a huge area for the personal comfort of just one person is a waste.

- Be especially careful to use HOT water wisely to avoid wasting energy as well as water. See that any leak or drip is fixed promptly. If there is a sprinkler or irrigation system, see that all sprinkler heads and pipes are in good repair. Make sure that sprinkler heads are adjusted or installed properly so that water falls on the areas that need it, not windows, buildings, walks, parking lots, etc. Set the sprinkler system so that watering is done in the early morning or late afternoon hours, when there is less breeze and heat and therefore less evaporation and more absorption by soil and plants. Be sure not to over water. "Stress" landscape plants and lawn just a little to develop roots that grow deeper in search of water. They'll be hardier and require less water to maintain.

Clean with your head, not just your hands—
in cleaning you can always do BETTER

➤There was a medium sized garage-type building that the resort manager imagined would be perfect for a boat house at the newly man-made lake site. The problem was, the little building was a few blocks away from where it had to be moved to, and the terrain was tough for vehicles. Bids were taken to jack up, load, haul, and place the building on the new site, and they ranged from $1200 to $1600 and two days' time. One of the lead cleaning people in the area heard about it, and you know a good cleaner is always eager to find a better way. In fact he had a "must be a better way" attitude and he lived up to it. So he ambled out and looked over the situation. Then he left a note for all the cleaning people to meet at the garage for root beer floats at 5:05 that evening (right after the regular shift). He promised that they would be there for only a few minutes. Once the gang of thirty was there, he had them circle the building and grab it at the base and heave-ho and lift it off the foundation. Then like a giant centipede, the building was moved to its new location in minutes. It was a great savings of time and money for the company, fun for the cleaners, and it took only $15 worth of root beer and ice cream.

➤The concrete floor in the telephone storeroom had been swept faithfully and well for twenty years. It took the janitor 2 hours, the set and accepted time for the job. This duty and time standard was passed from each new person to the next as the next twenty years rolled by. Eventually the building was expanded and the company didn't get around to hiring extra hands for the new larger area. A brand new cleaning person was assigned to the job, and he checked out the floor and talked to a supply salesman, who told him that concrete floors, once "sealed," could be dust mopped instead of using the dusty old push broom. A couple of evenings later, in a few hours and for a few dollars they sealed the storeroom floor. Now both the old and the new (double the size) floor could be done in 20 minutes, and that dustmop did a much better job with no dust. Plus a time savings of an hour and forty minutes a night. The cleaner got not just praise but a fat raise.

➤A college student was cleaning houses to get through college back when minimum wage was $1.15. It took 4 to 5 hours to clean the walls of the average room (bedroom or living room) in the average house, and for this you made about $7. The student had a large family to feed and needed to do better than bare survival at $1.40 an hour. So he found a better way. He found a dry sponge for quick surface cleaning and then a two-bucket system for faster, better washing, and later even came up with a wall cleaning machine. He was soon cleaning the walls of the average room in an hour and a half, then an hour. Finally in the right circumstances he could wash walls, woodwork, and all in half an hour. Since he was doing it by the bid instead of per hour, he was making $30 an hour on some jobs, in the days when lawyers and accountants were making $25 an hour.

➤A large recreation complex in the west had a total of 45 men and women working for them to do the cleaning, linen service, room setup and maintenance, snow shoveling, etc. One day because the 45 employees were forever whining and complaining about being overworked and needing help, the new operations manager sought alternatives. He found an enterprising young group of cleaners and offered them a chance. They did all the same work, only better, and smiling all the while, *with 15 people.*

➤It was cold up there in Alaska as Pierre daily swept the lot under the suspended grade school. It took almost all day and several brooms a year to round up all the fine beach sand, tossed litter and residue from vehicles. Pierre had actually developed sweeping muscles. He had 6 hours allotted for the job and it took 6 hours to do it. One day a visitor noticed the big lot, Pierre's big muscles, and those terribly worn and tortured brooms and told him about a machine that could do it better. It was a giant yard vacuum called a billy goat, a fast and inexpensive way to pick up all that sand and all those pop cans. Pierre suggested it to the boss and it was purchased. Today, Pierre cleans the area perfectly (even getting up the fine

Better means:

- a better quality job
- done faster
- and happier clients

dust that used to blow around and light on cars and windows) in a half hour per day! A good suggestion, a $600 machine, and a willing cleaner who wanted to do better saved that school district $25,000 a year in brooms and wages. Pierre got promoted to a position in the new school in town, and the management as well as the kids in the building loved him.

> **The bottom line of all these stories is, in cleaning you can always DO BETTER—and generally you get the reward!**

There is no magic involved in any of these stories, just something all of us can do, learn to work smarter and better: use newer and better tools, change our attitudes and schedules, maybe, organize the workload better, install more prevention measures and incorporate cleaning reducing design, get more help and cooperation from the mess makers (clients). All or any of these can change our jobs and lives for the better.

Cleaning what's there well, the way we've been told to do it is great. But figuring out how to clean it faster and better, or how to clean that new thing that's *going* to be there soon, is the mark of a real custodian. One well on the way up the promotional ladder.

How much can you do? How fast can you do it?

Cleaning was once work janitors just did—no science and no time standard. No one knew how long it should take, and wages were low enough that not many cared, either. A janitor was just let loose in a building... and whatever. Today cleaning is so competitive that a professional can tell you in advance exactly how long it will take to clean a small bank, school, or church, a whole factory, or a giant skyscraper. The cleaning industry now has generally accepted production rates for both in-house and contract cleaning, and you should be in line with them, able to do so much work in so much time. If it's taking you eight hours to do two or three hours' work, either the company's money or your job won't last very long. In the spirit of self-education I've included here a brief version of the time standards we use in my own company, computed from not only more than 35 years of our own experience but that of hundreds of other companies. Don't drown yourself in the janitor sink or hit up the boss for a raise if you are under or over these rates. Cleaning rates will vary somewhat with the situation—these are just averages, general guidelines for a quiet self-evaluation. Knowing where you are before the boss does is always an advantage.

Some factors that determine speed/quality in cleaning

AGE OF BUILDING

Older structures take longer to clean than new. Worn surfaces, dated HVAC units, ancient plumbing, wiring, and windows, ornate designs, high ceilings, and general inconvenience add about a 5 percent handicap.

SIZE

Larger buildings and facilities offer more crew flexibility and can be cleaned a little faster than usual.

LOCATION

Is it a rural, city, desert, jungle, or oceanside location? It has an effect on frequency, depreciation, etc.

CLUTTER FACTOR

How many "things" do you have to clean around, under, and through—how heavily furnished and decorated (and how just plain littered) is the area?

CONDITION

Whether something is in good repair, and how smooth, well painted or otherwise sealed the surfaces you have to clean are, is a big influence on cleaning speed.

POPULATION DENSITY

The number of people actively using an area has a great influence on the amount of soil, number of receptacles needed, schedule, workload.

USE/ACTIVITY

How much traffic, how many shifts does the area receive, and what products or activities are involved that create dust and debris?

HARD OR SOFT FLOOR?

If you handle it right, routine cleaning of carpet is about 10 percent faster than hard floors in areas that get steady use.

TRASH DISPOSAL

How easy is it to gather up the trash inside, and how much distance and effort is involved in dumping it outside?

FREQUENCY OF CLEANING

Whether something is cleaned seven days a week, three days a week, or once a

week makes a difference in the soil load and time it takes to clean it up.

EQUIPMENT

Do you have the biggest and best, or just a spray bottle and a rag to work with? It can affect cleaning speed up to 5 percent.

JANITOR STORAGE FACILITIES

Where your equipment and supplies are located, how much room there is for them, and how easily you can get to them is a big factor in time spent cleaning.

CONSTRUCTION

Is there construction going on in the area? Remodeling, additions, change-over can raise cleaning time by 20 percent.

How Much? How Fast?

The most accurate way to measure overall production rate is per hour: how many square feet of floor space or units of a specific type a person can do in one hour. This is usually computed by degree of difficulty: Light means it isn't too dirty, the area isn't crowded, and the surfaces and conditions involved are easy. Medium means average office or carpet or floor. Heavy means it's much tougher and more time consuming than usual and not easily accessible. (See charts on p. 42-44.)

Picking up Speed

As we head toward the 21st century, there is fierce competition in all jobs, and cleaning is no exception. There is a good life and good money in cleaning, and those who survive to enjoy and profit from the industry are those who make people like them because they do good work... FAST!

Speed is an important part of efficiency, and perfect cleaning work can be done fast, too, so don't let anyone kid you or convince you otherwise. If you need to pick up some speed in your cleaning performance, there are some simple things you can do/steps you can take to put yourself right up there with the supermen and women of the industry.

1. Like what you do. It's not always easy to force yourself to be fast or make yourself fast, but if you like what you do, you'll WANT to be fast, to do more and better of this thing you enjoy doing. So change or alter either you or it, but get in an area, position, schedule, whatever, that you really like, and then get on the starting line and GO!

2. Get and keep yourself in good health and habits. Out of shape, overweight, underslept, hung over, short-winded from smoking, etc., means we're always tired and late and behind. We just can't haul our fannies around as we need to, it's too hard or just plain impossible. Even if the mind says go, the body can't follow. So eat and sleep right and exercise, trim and tune up your body so that you feel good and can crank out the energy when you need to.

ing, or in the business. You'll learn how to do more, better and faster than you ever could from a book, pep talk, or video. Don't feel bad or lose your nerve because you can't perform to their level at first. Just get yourself side by side with them, asking questions, and working around them as much as you can… it will rub off!

6. Stretch yourself and take some risks… ask for more, reach for more, even if you don't get paid more for it… right now. You will if you keep stretching and getting faster, someone will steal you, make you an offer, promote you. Fast cleaners are rare and valuable, so learn to race the clock instead of watching it.

3. Have good equipment and supplies, keep up with modern methods and materials, and know (or learn) how to use them. The boss or the company may give us the basic know-how here, but to get that keen edge, that skill and smoothness, most of us need to do some further practice and training on our own. Speed is the cutting edge of better and WE are the only ones who can develop and cultivate it in ourselves.

4. Find out where you stand. Find out what the cleaning standards and speeds are, how much others are doing, how much of what you're doing other pros, your competitors, or other similar buildings are doing in how much time (see p. 42-44). Knowing what others are doing, what is expected, and what needs to be done ups our motivation—gives us a reason and a goal for getting better.

5. Work with and around the speed demons, the best in the build-

Watching old pros gives new patterns!

FOR MORE on how you can speed up your cleaning, read my other books of cleaning shortcuts and skills, especially *Is There Life After Housework?* and *The Cleaning Encyclopedia.*

TASK/JOB RATES	Easy, light building	Medium density building	Heavy full building
Trasher—Empty all trash, empty and wipe ashtrays, replace liners	41,000	36,000	25,000
Restrooms—Clean, service, sanitize restrooms completely	800	700	500
Vacuumer—Vacuum all carpets, detail around desk edges	15,000	10,000	7,000
Maid/Parlor work—Dust desks, ledges, spot clean, windows	35,000	24,000	18,000
Sweeper—Dustmop, spot clean, spillage	40,000	30,000	25,000
Floors, strip and wax (2 coats)	400	300	200
Hardwood floors—Prepare and seal (3 coats)	100	75	50
Carpet shampooing (extraction, truck mounted)	1,200	900	600
Carpet shampooing (rotary extraction)	800	600	400
Windows, large and unobstructed (squeegeed, per side)	3,600	2,000	1,500
Windows, small (squeegeed, per side)	600	800	200
Motel room (per maid daily)	18	15	12

These numbers are average square feet per hour that is cleaned/serviced

BUILDING TYPES

	Light	Medium	Heavy
Office building, Small—4,000 sq. ft. size, 3x week	2,500	2,000	1,500
Office building, Average to Small size—40,000 sq. ft. range, 5x week	4,000	3,000	2,800
Office building, Large high rise—300,000 sq. ft. range, 5x week	5,000	4,500	3,200
Branch bank—6,000 sq. ft. range, 5x week	3,500	2,500	2,000
Warehouse w/offices—1,000 sq. ft/office, 10,000 sq. ft. warehouse	10,000	7,500	6,000
Supermarket—35,000 sq. ft range 6 or 7x week	5,500	4,000	3,500
Department store—60,000 sq. ft. range 6 x week	7,000	5,000	4,000
Restaurant (not kitchen)—5,500 sq. ft. range, 7x week	2,800	2,500	2,000
Telephone/Commercial building—Equipment, building, few offices	8,000	6,000	4,000
Manufacturing plant—20 percent office, 80 percent open production space	5,000	3,500	2,500
Schools—any average size school	3,800	3,300	2,800
Churches—any average size and function church	6,500	5,000	4,500
College—each janitor to cover 30,000 sq. ft per day			

These numbers are average square feet per hour that is cleaned/serviced

AREA RATES

These are daily cleaning speeds, including all aspects of upkeep—light dusting, waxing, carpet care, trashing, vacuuming, spot cleaning, entrance area policing, etc.

	Light	Medium	Heavy
General offices	3,100	2,800	2,600
Executive offices	3,200	3,000	1,800
Corridors	6,200	5,800	5,300
Lobbies	3,800	3,600	3,300
Elevators	800	700	600
Cafeterias	2,000	1,700	1,500
Restrooms	800	600	500
Mechanical rooms	10,000	8,000	6,000
Auditoriums	3,800	3,300	2,800
Conference rooms	3,400	3,000	2,600
Data processing areas	4,000	3,800	3,500
Stairs	1,000	800	600
Parking garages	12,000	11,000	9,000
Telephone equipment	6,500	5,500	4,500

These numbers are average square feet per hour that is cleaned/serviced

Dashing Duty Disclaimer

How much can you do? How long will it take? Years ago we just took what time was available or assigned to clean and hurried up or filled up the gaps. Today, cleaning production is down to a computerized science. We **know** how much time is needed. I've computed an average here of how much/how fast so you can get a ballpark idea of your personal productivity. These rates will vary in extreme conditions (weather, age of facility, population density, etc.) but they are a good general summary of what is going on in the 90's. These figures are for your own information, to provide a guideline and comparison for pacing yourself. I can't be responsible for how (as far as quality goes) you apply them.

Some quick WHAT TO DO IFS

While cleaning many surprise situations come up. Trying to figure out a solution on the spot is risky. Some PREparation is smart, especially learning your company's policies for different circumstances. Here's my number one rule for any situation.

The Golden Rule of What to do if

Stay calm and in control; it's the secret of good sense and good results. You are always powerful when you're low key and controlled, in anything. Many think it impressive to raise your voice, snarl, show your temper, shake a fist, and so on... Wrong! Once you lose your cool, you are weak and ugly and usually unable to do anything but bluster and bully.

The Silver Rule of What to do if

Have a sense of humor. People say I find humor in everything—I even work humor into my funeral talks. It's easy to see the lighter side of things because it's there if you just look for it or think about it a minute. Just remember that I did say *sense* of humor. There are times to laugh inside only.... Whenever you can, first think humor; it will be a great aid to keeping calm. A smile, even a sick smile, helps!

Now some specifics: What to do if

You are criticized in public: Listen intently, accept it as criticism, just or unjust, and then think: Do I explain or respond now or later? Most of the time it is wise to just say, "Thank you, I appreciate your letting me know about this." It generally disarms the critic who will start looking for something to compliment you on. Take off or take care of the item next. Don't argue or defend yourself until the time and place are right. In public or in front of someone else is almost never right, because even if you win, you'll lose.

You find money: If it's near an identifiable place or person, even if it's just five pennies, I turn it all in. What if there is little hint or hope of finding the true owner? ("Would the loser of the $20 bill please form a line at the janitor closet....") If it's coins or a dollar or two, I don't worry about it. $5, $10, and up I put in an envelope, note on the envelope when and where I found it, and turn it in to the boss with my name.

You hear gossip: Don't listen to it and don't repeat it. It's that simple. It can do you zero good and will waste important brain cells and emotional space within you. What you hear or see in a place should stay in that place.

You have extra time: Read page 55 and then do it. Or stay out of sight!

You have to deal with drunkenness: Get a witness so that there are two or more of you, then talk gently to the person and find where they are headed or where they should be and do what you can to get them there. If there is even a hint of violence, abuse, or harassment, call security or the police.

You get locked out: You went out to dump the trash and left the keys inside. Embarrassing, and you are still out. If you're uniformed while beating on doors, the police generally won't haul you away. Trying to crawl or break back in is always a loser. Lower your pride and call the boss or someone with a key. A lesson, ALWAYS keep the key on you, and stay aware of it, just like a gun or a watch.

Someone else's mess is drifting onto your territory: You have your yard and steps and dock clean, but the neighbor has forty Siberian elms that drop off two hundred tons of seeds, pods, and leaves every year. And the nearby motel has no lawn, so the guests all walk their dogs over to your lawn. In situations like this I first sit down with the offenders in

person and let them know it's a real problem and ask what can we do about it? If no results, then put it in writing and make a follow-up call if necessary. If still no results, they're probably not sensitive enough to understand anything but police enforcement of any pertinent ordinances… or a lawsuit. But exhaust all possible alternatives first.

You break something: It will happen, especially when you're new in the business. I knocked over a china closet loaded with antique china, broke some choice desk decorations, and buffered my way through a few baseboards. The impulse is to run; the right thing is to pay. Don't sneak past it. First clean it up (don't put it back together and lay it down so that when they pick it up they'll think they broke it… tempting, huh?). Clean it up and leave a note, or if others are there, inform them right away that you broke it. "I accidentally damaged the ____ while cleaning. What can I do to get it restored / replaced?" Often at this point people say, "Oh, don't worry, that's just one less thing to clean," and you are off the hook. They may actually be relieved to be rid of it and now admire your honesty.

You have more work or assignments than you can do: Make sure you really do have more than you can do before presenting the dilemma to the boss. S/he might say, "Well, your replacement can do it all." Don't go to them with a problem to solve; you are the one doing the work (or trying to get it all done), so figure out what solution would take care of it and go to the boss with that. It may be a better or bigger vacuum, or maybe a switch in schedule might alleviate the problem. Think, think, and think again before whining. Then iron it out quickly, and **never** whine in public.

You are feeling bored and burned out on your job and it's showing: We don't burn out (most of us haven't been lit yet), we bore out. Again I wouldn't complain to the boss and ask him to make you a happy cleaner. You better size it up first, figure out what you don't like and what you would like (maybe an area or duty change, maybe a different partner). Do all you can to **correct it yourself** first. Ninety percent of job dissatisfaction is with ourselves, not the job.

After you've made every effort to correct it and still the job gives you the blahs, I'd visit with the boss about it and ask for help. It doesn't do anyone any good to stick with a job that turns you off—it hurts the job and it decays you. Sometimes a change of profession is needed, nothing wrong with that. Instead of quitting, you might call it repotting.

You invent something: You think about it and you dream about it—something that makes cleaning easier, faster, or cheaper. But you never do anything about

it. Many cleaners come up with good tools and new ideas, and many big companies are budgeting for and dying to get new things. Trouble is they aren't mind readers. You have options when you are blessed with a new idea…

a. Patent, develop, and manufacture it yourself

b. Sell the idea

c. Make a joint deal with a big manufacturer

I feel that big companies are trustworthy and I will send ideas in to them, along with a copyrighted drawing, and hope they like it. It might cost you a million to tool up for and sell an item, while someone like 3M, Sears, Clarke, or Rubbermaid can plug it right into their system. Best for both of you. In cleaning magazines you can find the address of nearly every cleaning-related business and manufacturer. Approach one company at a time. Pick out the best one and write a letter to the product development office explaining the idea briefly and go from there. If you feel it's hot, then get an appointment and go in person. All inventors will tell you it took effort, but then again, there is satisfaction.

You see a seduction: Ah yes, we cleaners in quiet tennis shoes have embarrassed many bosses and their secretaries. We constantly run across the scene or sound or the evidence of both the hanky and the panky and this is one time it is definitely best to fade out as gracefully as possible and let the event fade from our minds and never escape from our lips. Love and lust are both very personal things, and only if the situation involved is clearly detrimental to the health, wealth, and welfare of the building and its occupants would I report it confidentially to the boss or an authority you feel comfortable confiding in.

Your equipment is a joke, crappy: First make sure, before you open your mouth, that the condition in question is other than your doing. If you broke or ruined it and start groaning and moaning about it, you'll only be hanging yourself. You need to get the boss or buyer to look at the problem and understand how it's affecting the job and you. Then tactfully have the alternative ready when asked, "Well what does a new machine cost?" Do this very carefully—if you already have a written quote and the order half filled out, the bosses will resent your presumptuousness. They love to be the initiators and feel that buying it was their doing, not yours. Let them have that, graciously, as long as the situation gets fixed.

You are accused of stealing: This is common and for every time it's said out loud—"The janitor did it"—400 people have thought it. I believe that janitors and cleaners are among the most trustworthy people on earth, but because we have a key and we're there, when something is gone, the janitor is naturally the first one the finger is pointed at.

Just because we expect this and are used to it, doesn't mean we should accept it, so immediately take steps to defuse it. Listen to the charges, then immediately take the offense and ask them when and where as well as what. Once I have all the info, I fix a beady eye on the accusers and make it clear that since this is my area, I

know what's what, having taken care of it for 20 years. I've been here all along and have the keys (I always hold them up at this point) and if I'd wanted whatever's missing, I'd have taken it 19 years ago when I was hard up. I tell them I've never stolen a thing in my life, and if I ever started, I'd start with one of the company cars or planes (not a calendar or calculator). Then I volunteer to help them find the thief. Another important defusing factor here is heading it off. Long before an uncomfortable situation like this ever occurs, I'm always sure to turn in things and report them, etc. This builds a reservoir of honest acts and trust so that when something is missing, they don't have the nerve to accuse me or even think of me; in fact, my boss will defend me. That's the best of all worlds!

You witness or know of thievery taking place on the job. The bottom line here is that you're not helping the thieves, your company, or yourself by looking the other way and ignoring stealing of any kind. Stealing is wrong, and it destroys everything we believe in and work for in our lives and families. Be loyal to the one who pays your wages, not to a friend who is dishonestly taking money or property. Report it.

You see someone breaking the rules: All companies have rules and policies, for one purpose—the basic preservation of the company. I know we're all born rule benders, but breaking them is something else. If you see rule breaking and policy violation, it too is something you are obligated not to ignore. My approach on this is to visit with the breaker and make sure he knows his action is contrary to policy. If he continues to break rules, it could mean breaking the company that provides a living for us all. Report it discreetly.

You become aware of drug use on the job: Oh, for the good old days when catching someone smoking a cigarette butt behind the barn was the worst scenario. Always report drug violations, because they affect the safety and security of the entire building and even your job and life.

You have a bad case of black heelers: You could kill them, but safer and more kindly conduct is to find the soul with the soles leaving the black marks and kindly persuade him to save those shoes for a sunny day outside. Surprising how people will respond when you ask them nicely to help you solve a problem.

You find something personal left out: If you put it away, be sure to leave a note on it saying… "Found your wallet lying on the desk, put it in the file cabinet. Aloha, Jack the Janitor." If you find something and there's no place to put it safely, put it in a clean sack and lock it in the closet; then call or leave a note that you have it so that the owner won't panic. Whatever you do, don't take it out of the

building. If someone sees it or notices it missing before you can say anything, conclusions might be drawn negative to your integrity.

The phone rings: Make sure you have a policy on this *before* it rings—it can be dynamite. Some of us working in small operations are told to answer calls, because we work Saturday afternoon or evenings when the place is closed. Sometimes the policy is to let it ring, yet you have a wife about to go into labor and you're at K-Mart or a closed bank doing the floor. You answer, and it isn't your wife, it's the big boss—big trouble!

The public fiddles with the thermostat: Of course the place is freezing or boiling and 400 calls come in about it (to the boss first, of course). This makes us all look incompetent. When we check, we find a toothpick or hunk of gum stuck in there to screw up the automatic temperature control. You can stand guard, but they'll beat you every time. The final cure is installing a tamper proof unit. (Far better than an announcement telling everyone to stop it, or now 800 people, including those who never even thought about it before, will be monkeying with the heat.) Now you do want to announce that the new unit is set for the most comfortable temperature as per the average, and if that's too cold or too hot, then please wear a sweater or take one off.

You get contradictory directives:

Ah yes, they come and go and never end, conflicts—the schedule and the boss tell you to do one thing and someone else tells you to do another, in a different way, at a different time. The husband gives you one instruction and the wife another, one manager of the building wants the door closed, the other tells you to leave it open. You can't do both, and doing either one will mean an enemy.

In any conflicts, I follow my boss, my immediate supervisor, or the directions in the schedule. The minute I find out there's a conflict, however, I bring it up in a positive manner. I inform the new or initiating party what my duties and directives are concerning the matter at hand and kind of let them be the ones to tell me to disobey my boss. They seldom if ever will. Be nice to them, like "Would you like me to talk to my boss about it? Maybe we can work it out your way. I'd sure like to help you anyway I can." Handled this way, contradictory orders can win you friends and respect.

Handling
EMERGENCIES

We all go to work planning on a normal day, and most of the time roll along as expected, but when something unexpected happens, you'll never guess who the first person to get called is... right! **You**. When you assume the position of care-

taker for a building, for some reason you inherit the position of information center and that means emergency center, too. Being human like everyone else, and sharing their fears of fire, flood, earthquake, tornado, etc., your first impulse will be like everyone else's... RUN! But you, like the stewardesses of the airways, are going to have to traffic the situation when the time comes. People will turn to you, seek you out, and let you tell them what they should do. You have to do something, and for everyone's sake it should be the right thing.

Whether a situation is serious or nonserious, if it's serious to the person panicked about or reporting it, then you better treat it as serious. I remember once hearing a telephone building filled with screams, genuine, sincere, full-volume screams, and women came pouring out the door like bees out of a hive, holding their hair with one hand and their blouse tops with the other. Whatever it was had unquestionably gotten the full attention of quite a few women—some were in sheer terror. Finally from the babbling I determined that a bat was attacking them. When we moved into the room for the

carpet), then make sure you use a nice big official barricade.

A fall: Gets my attention before a volcano, earthquake, or presidential visit! Even if it's only a minor fall, rush to the scene and take over. Encourage the victims not to move, to stay still until they and you are sure they are okay. Most people are embarrassed at a moment like this and will try to get up and act as if nothing happened, even if they have a broken back. Call nearby staff for help— your boss if possible. If there is any chance it's serious, any chance at all, call an ambulance. Better to be charged with a false call than face the liability for not calling.

Next, whatever caused the fall, quickly pick it up or cover it so that the ambulance crew won't be carrying themselves back. If it's something like a slick floor, hole in the rug, etc., report it and correct it immediately, or as soon as possible.

Be sure to record the reason for the fall—the record these days is more important than a bank note.

Fire: We all get plenty of preparation for this one, but when it actually happens, we have to think and scramble for phone numbers and extinguishers, etc. Keep the fire plan fresh in your mind so that you can follow it. Again, taking action, even for a false alarm, is smart.

confrontation, there wasn't a soul left, and clinging to a side of a fluorescent fixture was a trembling, scared-half-to-death, innocent little 4-inch bat. The tiny critter had single-handedly put the long distance division of an entire state out of commission in seconds. Yes, sure we wanted to laugh, but instead sober and serious faced, we clunked the animal into a box so that we could take it outside and turn it loose. The women were practically climbing the walls when we walked by with it in the box. To me that wasn't an emergency, but it was to the building.

In an emergency, real or not, you need to be the brave parent of the hour and take action, face it and handle it. I can't outline every possible emergency here, but your building will have emergency plans and you must have the good sense to handle almost anything that comes along. Here are general guidelines for a few of the most common "maydays."

A spill: Barricade it! If you can't wipe it up instantly, all the way to DRY, then barricade it. If you don't have an official yellow-colored barricade, then use a person, a chair, or anything that can easily be seen and not easily walked over. Leaks, coffee spills, vomit, food, anything that spills is an instant hazard to people and places if left unguarded and uncleaned. So barricade it; then clean it up. If it has to be left a while to dry afterward (such as

Choking: Get help from someone with first aid experience with choking. In a large building there are almost sure to be people who know what to do. Identify them ahead of time so that you can find help fast when you need it. If there's no one on the spot who can help, call the first aid squad. (You might consider taking a first aid course yourself—it's good to know exactly what to do at moments like this.)

Heart attacks: Make the victim comfortable and call an ambulance. Then make sure the front of the building, etc., is clear for easy access. Sometimes the ambulance makes it there in 5 minutes and it takes 15 to find the way into and through the building. Set up a path or course to the victim, and station people at doors to make sure the way *stays* clear.

Fight: People mad enough to fight are crazy enough to turn on you or shoot or club you to death, too. Call security or the police quickly and then keep people clear of the problem.

Robbery: There's a good chance this could happen to you. If you can slip off and call the police or security, do it. If not, cooperate—a few beads and bills are a good trade for no bullets. Big mouths and big ideas during robberies generally mean bigger trouble. Just observe carefully and cooperate.

Blizzard/Snowed in: No one emerges more important during these circumstances than the custodian. Few are going to do anything but sit and whine or wait to be "plowed out." During storm season we want to be on a snow alert and be prepared to walk or hitch a ride early to our post. Walk or run, but get there—with your snow tools!

Earthquake: Follow earthquake safety measures and then stay and help others. You are a custodian—obligated to worry about other lives before your own.

The main thing to remember in dealing with emergencies and people in buildings is that few people, not even bosses and owners, know where "things" are (power switches, shut-off valves, phone numbers, emergency gear, etc.). You learn fast that in times of trouble, the custodian is the #1 source of solutions. YOU! So in short, you don't get to muddle through emergencies of any kind... you HANDLE THEM!

No matter how terrified you may be in any emergency, remain calm and don't show it. If the janitor panics, the cause will be lost. You need to keep in control because you know where everything is.

Most of the buildings you work in will have emergency measures all charted. It's your job to know them and think them through and thus be in a frame of mind and position to respond positively if and when emergencies occur. Remember always when dealing with the public—**advised is better than surprised!**

Deliveries

When something is delivered and no one knows where it goes, it's easiest to find "the janitor." We are often the only ones around when UPS, Fed Ex, the 2,000 concrete blocks for the new addition, or some other important delivery arrives. The delivery person's goal is to be rid of the merchandise and get someone else to sign for and take responsibility for it.

If you don't know the policy on this, or there is none, **stop right now and ask your supervisor.** Get official confirmation of your duty to sign for and accept deliveries, where to put them, etc. Most buildings will not want you to accept such things.

When you do accept a parcel, write the time of arrival on the receipt they give you. Always take a moment to count the packages to make sure what they say has been delivered is there. If the count is short, write on all copies of the receipt, "I received only ____ packages," then your name and date.

Ask the delivery person if it's **perishable.** We all know that flowers, ice cream, or live chicks need immediate attention,

but many things can be ruined by cold, heat, time (yes, even just one weekend!), or being set on the wrong end and need to be dealt with accordingly. Read any warning signs on the box and be sure to stay alert to this.

If you're not sure where the parcel goes, lock it up or give it to the building manager. Never leave things out or up against the door for the addressee to pick up when he comes in. It may be confidential, or it may even disappear.

Construction and Remodeling: You're Part of It (whether you want to be or not!)

You can count on it. Once in a while (it seems like all the time) the buildings we clean will have construction, remodeling, or repair jobs going on. You'd swear platoons of big-hoofed equipment and material-dragging gorillas are determined to pulverize and pollute your serene building. You'll find sheet rock mud on the toilet seat, spilled coffee and half-eaten sandwiches lodged in between piles of boards and rolls of plastic. Nails left behind everywhere to be run over and flipped around by the mower and clink through your vacuums, and there will be lumber bands and roofing tile pieces and chunks of wood and tar paper scraps everywhere. The builders are always popping the circuit breakers and tromping through the place to find something and

1. First, find out what's going to happen and when, for how long, and how much it's going to interfere with the cleaning. Then double all that is told to you and you'll be prepared—maybe.

2. Go make arrangements to handle the coming assault of debris and extra people, the temporary loss of space and access, need for extra toilet paper, and for people to know who has the keys to what, etc.

3. *Make friends with the contractors and the crew.* It's marvelous how much of their own mess they will clean up once they realize you're a human and want to get home to your spouse and family, too!

4. Suggest a parking area for the gang.

5. Provide extra waste containers. Make sure they're the kind with lids.

of course they leave the electricity off afterward so that everything in the refrigerator spoils. They will rope off and occupy the best and closest parking areas for months (seems like years). They stream in and out of the place, carrying tools and supplies back and forth, tearing up the doors and door casings. They fill the dumpster with ripped-out wall sections so that there's no room for your trash (you have to pile it by the side and it breaks open and blows all over the county at night). They also pile up pyramids of containers and materials that you have to sweep and walk around forever. They rob and ruin half the stuff in your janitor closet. And worst of all, this inconvenience to everyone in the building will often be vented on you, the maintenance person...

Ahhhh, but that's life in big buildings as well as little ones. And the truth is that the work they're doing is probably going to better things for everyone, especially you. Once you get the snarl out of your lip, the only choice is to cooperate fully and do everything you can to help speed them up and control the extra cleaning caused while they're about.

There's going to be a ton of extra trash from three sources: 1. things they rip up and destroy getting out; 2. packaging and packing containers (and scraps) from all the new material coming in; and 3. personal garbage from lunches, snacks, smoking, gum chewing, etc. The big plastic "Brute" containers are inexpensive and easy to place around. Remember, you're going to get all the trash anyway, and if you provide a receptacle, they may put it in. Then you won't have to round it up, just haul it off.

You'll also want to alert the manager to call the garbage company to let them know that you'll need more frequent dumping or more bins, or maybe both.

6. Buy extra mats. You can usually expense them off on the construction job and they will without question be a lifesaver for everyone in the building and the HVAC. They'll prevent falls, keep the floors from getting ground up by mortar and sand, cut down the noise a little, etc. Long runners are smartest. In some cases I like to keep to the standard 4' x 8' size or smaller so that they can be rolled up and moved or stored without a crane and kinked neck.

7. Control the keys to your closet. Otherwise you'll have a real disaster on your hands. Those people are going to need water and brooms and everything. When the "Jesse James Construction Company" moves in, spray bottles, towels, buckets, mops, and rolls of towels will disappear out of there like mad. And when you try to find their whereabouts, you'll never meet more pure, innocent men than those burly builders. I'd pull out an old loaner vacuum and hide my good one, because they will vacuum up the ends of two-by-fours and broken shovel handles as well as all those bent nails. You either need to

hide your equipment itself or hide the keys or something, because rest assured, they will "nail" your tools and it will never be the same. And they leave gunk (heaven only knows whether it's mud, paint, mastic, or barf) in the bottom of the sink drain, and it will set up like epoxy.

8. Most importantly, cleverly, subtly (prior to and during the siege) let management know that any construction increases the cleaning workload/trash load around 20 percent and that you are breaking your butt to handle it without a moan or groan (an audible one, at least).

Impressive (and productive) things to do when you aren't busy!

Most of the time we all have plenty to do, maybe more than plenty. But I've hardly ever seen a cleaning job where, some time or other, everything required and scheduled isn't finally caught up. Never translate this as time to loaf. When you're being paid, you must be working, not hiding out or stalling around till quitting time. I promise you this is something that makes a real difference in how you are viewed by clients and bosses, as well as how you feel about yourself and your job. Things that you do on your own—**"taking the initiative,"** as this virtue is called—are the mark of a true professional, a real man or woman, a champion. When you get caught up, don't just take "break time," disappear, or visit your life and time away, even if it is legal or okay. Sitting around anytime tabs you as unambitious or lazy. The big-

gest rut or downfall of a cleaning professional is getting the regular duties so ingrained in your speed and thinking, getting so adjusted to them, that extra or more can't be considered or worked into your schedule when you do have the time and opportunity.

There are all kinds of things you can do at slow moments to improve your job and make the boss love you. You'll hear others gripe and moan that doing more than bargained for and agreed upon is just allowing the company to take advantage of you. Wrong, wrong. You are always the ultimate winner when you do more. This kind of extra push on your own is one of the finest and fastest ways to get noticed, promoted, and moved into leadership positions.

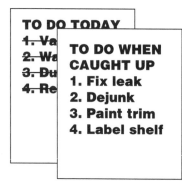

Both we cleaners and the company all have our lists and I don't want to make yours because I don't know your building or schedule. But just to give you the idea, let me share my own "standby list" with you. I always keep a notebook handy as I clean and work along, and I write down things I see that need done so I'll remember what they are when I happen to have the time.

Things to do when you are caught up

Public relations
Visit and get to know customers and clients, bosses and vendors, students and teachers. Do all you can to make and promote peace, help them, express appreciation to them, etc.

Preventive maintenance
Look over the whole building or area closely, look for repairs that are needed and potential structure failures.

Catch things that are worn before they break. Overhaul units with heavy hours on them. Check belts, handles, washers, etc., and replace as necessary. See that all vacuums and floor machines are in condition to function perfectly. Make upgrading plans.

Dejunk
Go through all storage rooms and closets under your department's control and clean out inactive, obsolete, broken, unneeded stuff.

Self-train
Sit down for a few minutes or hours and watch a video or filmstrip, catch up on professional magazines.

Share the work
If someone in the building is down or behind, join in a group effort and get it all done in an hour or two. Extra hands make lighter work and lasting friends.

Clean up equipment and label it

What equipment is ever clean enough? Splash marks and nicks on machines and tools project a sloppy image—a few hours can correct it all.

Labeling your tools with your department or company name is a good idea, too. You can go a step further here and paint, decorate, or personalize your cleaning tools to make them sharp and attractive. Use your imagination.

Give a lecture or teach a class

For a local club, city, or church group. They always need help, and you can let them in on some professional ways to speed up and improve maintenance.

Repair leaky plumbing fixtures

Do those little things that never get done

Replace burned-out light bulbs, label all panel and fuse boxes, fix that sticking drawer, unjumble the hardware or spare parts collection, etc. You should have a standby or request list ready for moments like these.

Do frequency work

Annual frequency work (like cleaning light fixtures, ceiling tile, air circulation vents, washing doors) always seems to crowd up when it falls due. Getting some of this done ahead of time keeps us aggressively progressive.

Improve safety

Tighten all those things (like stair railings and hinges) that need tightening. Get rid of, or pad, the head and shin bumpers. Mark chemicals as required, update all MSDS sheets and review OSHA requirements.

Fix up, paint, and organize janitor closets and other storage facilities.

Do whatever you can to reduce the need for cleaning and repair work

Look around, think, and evaluate things. Make sure all areas under your control have adequate litter and waste receptacles. Paint, seal, varnish, panel, or otherwise cover surfaces (such as raw concrete floors) that absorb stains and are hard to wash, dust, or clean. Make sure all chair and table legs have good protective covers. Caulk and weather-strip to reduce air and dirt leakage into buildings. Make the tops of doors smooth and dustable by sanding them and giving them a couple coats of polyurethane. Do what you can to make sure all cooking areas and other sources of airborne grease and dirt are well vented.

And then there are those "dream" ideas we all have

Don't let them float away—be sure to write them down and save them. They aren't as strange or ridiculous as they might appear when we first think of them. They are inventions the world needs, problems that need to be solved, or things you've wanted to do. Or just answers to some recent on-the-job challenges.

We seem to think some magic "they" out there invents everything and brings it to pass. Not so; even the most famous invention started with a person just like you who saw a need and tried to think of a way to fill it.

A few minutes spent here to find a new idea, a better way, will help keep the maintenance industry interesting and attractive to you. The following is my list—it may give you some ideas for getting started.

- Invent a better baseboard
- Find ways to reduce vandalism
- Ways to keep food and drink out of work areas or restrict them to the cafeteria, etc.
- To keep gum out of buildings
- Make office users more sensitive to cleaning and maintenance problems
- Design maintenance-free materials, surfaces, and structures
- Ways to reduce turnover in our industry
- Invent cleaning games
- Find better ways to store stuff
- Devise a standard policy to solve vending machine messes
- Invent a small, portable, self-contained mop bucket
- The perfect stain removal kit
- Mess preventives for "big bash" events
- The ideal customized janitor closet
- The perfect janitor closet bulletin board
- Engineer/organize a "cleaning day" that involves clients
- Invent the perfect incentive program for custodians
- Design buildings or offices that allow robot cleaning

Make your own list and keep it handy as *you* go along in your cleaning work.

Then, **go ask** for work. Think of the fun of seeing the shocked look on the face of the building's biggest complainers when you bounce into their offices with a smile (fake it if you have to) and say "Mr. Snaggletooth, I have 30 minutes of clear time. Is there anything I can clean or take care of just for you?" You've done the ultimate in PR and won a friend for life. And he'll probably put you on to something that really bugs him and helps you as well as the company to fix. Make another trip back the next day to tell him you got it taken care of and thanks—and guess what, I'll bet you lose the biggest complainer in the building. Repeat, if the first time or second time doesn't do it. It might take seventy times seven, but it'll work eventually, and wow will the place be shaped up! Complainers are generally also the biggest braggers, and before long they'll be telling everyone around what a good person you are!

P.S. *Be sure to do these little extra, over-and-above jobs out in the open, in public view. (Even the scriptures tell you to let your good works be known.) If no one sees, be sure, by note or word, that the people in the area or the boss knows that an extra effort was made for them. This says "I appreciate my job" and good PR like this on your part means people will appreciate you, and appreciation is the best reward going.*

CHAPTER 4

GETTING PEOPLE TO LIKE YOU:
Public Relations for the Pro Cleaner

You clean for...

You clean around...

You clean up after...

You clean up before...

You are appreciated by...

You get paid by...

YOU HAVE TO PLEASE...

PEOPLE

If there's one saying you want to engrave on your cleaning bracelet and in your mind and manners, it is...

> **"I can't clean well enough
> to please people
> if they don't like me."**

If you hate human society, don't get along with people easily, or have any obnoxiousness in your blood, you won't be happy or last long in the cleaning industry. You can't clean well enough to please people if they don't like you.

It took me (and others) many years to finally learn the value of being liked and wanted on the job. As soon as customers, clients, and the public recognize that you are a human being who has feelings and needs like other people, you've come a long way toward becoming a successful cleaner who enjoys his or her job and gets raises and recognition. How is it done?

Making people know you exist, that you are there, and count for something? Well it just doesn't happen. Bosses can command people to treat you well, but that's like telling someone who can't stomach you to fall in love with you. You have the burden here, you have to be the one to let your actions leap out and say, "Here I am, a pro cleaner. I'm working hard, doing a great job for you, and I like to be treated with respect." Here are some proven attention getters, which surprisingly few cleaners know or use.

1. Learn and remember names, even if they haven't learned yours in forty years and it's there in four-inch letters on your uniform. Take the offensive and learn the name of the principal people you work for and around. And know whether to call them Mr. or Ms. or Miss. I prefer to call people "Sir" and "Ma'am"—it's dignified.

2. Grow thick skin: Sure people will pick on you about petty things and complain about a couple of fly footprints after you've worked three days around the clock cleaning up an unnecessary mess they caused. But just smile and nod and say, "Thanks, how can I help?"

3. Take a humble parking place. Don't hog the closest and best place, even if you're there first and have earned it. Parking out under the trees across the lot instead, where the birds can poop on your car says, "There, people, I left the best spot for you. I'm happy to walk a little extra to serve you." They'll love you for it.

4. Don't smoke. If you can't make it through the day without one, then smoke in a totally private place. Smoking is fast becoming the mark of an addicted, un-

healthy, environmentally irresponsible person. Practicing a messy habit like smoking while you clean degrades you, even if your work is immaculate. Keep personal habits out of public view. Yes, you have a right to eat, drink, sleep, and take breaks like anyone else, but a professional never allows any of this to be a public spectacle. Smoking on the job is a poor policy, and anti-clean.

5. Confine your eating to a private place, too. A cleaner who is dumping trash or polishing a desk while crunching an apple or sipping coffee will irritate people. Even setting your sandwich or whatever down nearby is messy and ill mannered.

6. Don't use private telephones, or better still, call from a public phone on your break. There's something about a cleaner using a desk phone that really bugs people. Why may be hard to understand, but regardless, it does, so don't do it. People in offices get enough aggravation without our adding to it.

7. No personal radios, even with earphones. It's not just an issue of safety, of what might happen while you're distracted by a radio. Having a radio around projects an "I'm not really too interested in the job" attitude. It might be your fa-

vorite music, Willie singing through his nose or Pavarotti vibrating his tonsils out, but it won't be everyone's favorite. People will hate you for it. Leave those radios home. Doing any job with earphone music is suicide. You can't hear motor sound changes, warnings, phones, orders or instructions, danger signs, etc.

8. Crude or profane language. At home on the ranch "s__t" may be a common word (even the minister uses it). But on the job, and for that matter anywhere in public, there's no place for expressions like this, especially around a clean business. A four- or five-letter expletive every other breath, or constantly taking the Lord's name in vain, will offend even fellow swearers. I've heard custodians say "Well that's their tough luck if they don't like my language." Wrong, it's your tough luck, and if you use bad language on the job, you watch, your luck will get tougher and tougher.

9. Never moan and groan publicly about injustice, even if someone lets a pet pee on your freshly shampooed rug. We cleaners are great grumblers at times, and true, we do have plenty to grumble

about. Just don't do it in front of anyone, ever. Half the people don't want to hear your problems and the other half think you're getting what you deserve.

10. Noise!! Make little. Avoid excess noise. It's natural for you to want everyone to know and see you working. But being noisy is the wrong way to go about it! People hate clanging, banging, squeaking wheels, etc. **Clean softly and carry a big mop.** Nothing is worse than custodians, waiters, or maids competing in a slamming and clanking contest. I remember once paying $3000 for a hotel conference room and during the presentations, dinners, etc., the cleaning staff came charging by, vacuums wailing at top volume, metal baskets rattling, not even aware of any of us there. Cleaning noise really irritates people. They may not say anything, but mentally they're writing you right off their list. Whistling and singing, believe it or not, are included here, too. You might feel like breaking into song or yodel as you clean through the airport, church, hotel, office, hospital, or wherever, but be careful. People are trying to concentrate, converse, or rest, so make sure you're in a people-free place before humming a tune.

11. Odors and smells: Minimize or eliminate them. We secretly like cleaning odors to whack the public on the head and give evidence of our work, but they're not too likely to enjoy being blasted with ammonia or pine fragrance. Keep the cleaning smells (and your own body aromas, too, from Brut to "overdue for a bath") unobtrusive. We get used to disinfectant odor, solvents, sickening urinal block scent, over-perfumed dust treat, aerosol propellants and more, but those around us don't. Think. Some have aller-

gies, and the slightest odor or irritation can send them into convulsions. If you have to do a smelly job, announce it in advance, "Hi folks, I'm Don Aslett, the janitor here, and I need to sanitize these crates. There might be a little odor, but it won't last long." This will go a long way toward preserving a good contract relationship.

12. Honor others' privacy (see p. 68).

13. On the job, be a lady... be a gentleman.
At all times treat others with respect and courtesy, and strive to promote good feelings between yourself and coworkers, bosses, clients, and customers. They will not only love you but help you in your cleaning quest!

14. Have a rapid response rate.
Delays have a fatal effect on PR. The second someone needs or requests something, answer immediately and arrange it right away. Other professions may be able to put off work, but we can't. Because most of our job involves things that are highly visible, smellable, and potentially dangerous. How quickly you respond will have a big effect on the future quality of your public relations.

15. Offer before they ask.
Beat people to the punch, offer to do something before they ask you to do it. Watch this work like magic. You know they're going to ask, so do it first. Then the accomplishment is in your court!

16. Practice aggressive appreciation.
Seek out and thank anyone for positive acts of cleaning or helpfulness. Write notes, and publicly praise people who pitch in, pick up, and help out. Be on the lookout for opportunities to give a pat on the back—we all appreciate them.

17. Highlight your finds!
A good pro doesn't play finders-sweepers. Inevitably, everyone who works in the place you service will lose something or leave it behind. You find it, and since we cleaners are among the most trustworthy people around, you just take it to the boss or to Lost and Found. But you're really losing some mileage if you don't make a little bigger deal out of it than that. Make up a little "Found" tag for things like this, with your name on it, and tie it to the article and fill in the tag.

I found this _____ (what it is and when and where you found it) while cleaning the area. Sincerely, Jake

When the item is placed in their hands, they're always so happy but never know who to thank. Here you give them someone (after all, even the scriptures say "let your good works be known"). This builds good feelings and friendship and it'll make *you* feel pretty good when they thank you for your honesty in front of the whole company at lunch. And of course, that woman who got her purse back will tell everyone in town, and boy will you have a reputation! A well-deserved one.

The NUMBER ONE rule of public relations in cleaning

We clean to make things look good, keep them sanitary, and keep people happy. As a pro, you need to know whether you've accomplished this, but if you want to get into real problems, just ask that stupid question of clients or bosses:

"Well, how does it look?"

Ninety-nine percent of the time, when you ask someone a cleaning evaluation question like this, they will *look* for something wrong. They expect the positive, take it for granted, so if it's good, it isn't reportable. So they'll quickly search for a flaw (and generally find one, in my work or yours) and hit you with it. Everyone in the world has an opinion about personal judgment items like food, weather, mar-

riage, and cleaning. Some people would consider a place with dead flies and flung spaghetti hanging off the fixtures clean, while others will rave like lunatics when a single moth whisker is left on a 30 foot square executive desk. Once someone finds fault in your work, even if 98 percent of it is perfect, they will remember the negative and bring up the 2 percent forever. They aren't trying to be mean either; it's just human nature and the universal reaction to cleaning, edging always to the negative.

This took me many of years to learn. I had to know how they liked my work, but coming right out and asking "Well, how does it look?" was cleaning suicide. Finally I realized that I was the pro and I *knew* how clean or dirty something was. So I started out on the offensive instead of the defensive. I found out what I wanted to know, yet kept the client/boss positive and constructive and helping me get better instead of looking for faults.

For example, you work on an old stained carpet for hours and get it clean; however, not all the stains are removable, and you can't grow the worn-off pile back on the carpet…

Wrong: "Well, J. B., we cleaned your carpet, how does it look?"

Right: "Well, J. B., I personally spent four hours on your carpet. All of the dirt and all the removable stains came out beautifully. Some of the worn spots do show up now that it is thoroughly clean and the permanent damage-stains show a bit. Short of scissors we did everything a pro can do."

Then wait for their reply. You bet it will be "**Thanks.**"

A real pro cleaner has to know how things are, but seldom asks. They tell—and ask for added suggestions.

Another example:

Wrong: "Good morning, Mr. Squinteye. We deep cleaned the entire bank, how's it look?"

(You and I know darned well that if Superman cleaned it, one or two little things would be missed or left and Squinteye will know, and have them ready right now on his note pad to chew you out. Beat him to the punch like a real pro should.)

Right: "Good morning, Mr. Squinteye. We probably handled 2000 different items and areas deep cleaning your place here and it turned out well. A couple of tough places I worked on personally for hours and finally got them. I imagine we might not have gotten everything back exactly in order yet. You could help us, if you know of any little things. Thanks for the help."

Socializing with the clients

Again, we have a tough line to draw when it comes to "being friendly" with customers and the public while we clean. This is a touchy business, because bosses get mighty irritated if they see you leaning on your broom or stopping the mopping to chat. And clients can get almost equally irritated if they think you're cold and standoffish. It's a fine line between friendly and obnoxious. We all hear "Janitors stand around and talk too much" almost as often as we hear "Boy, s/he sure is unfriendly, hardly gives you the time of day." Kind of a darned if you do and darned if you don't situation, without a clear-cut, black and white answer. We all know the friendly janitor who's like an overgrown St. Bernard. He jumps on everyone, sets his heavy paws on them, and wags his "tales." I've seen janitors like this actually help office production because those workers rushed and darted everywhere at top speed to avoid running into George, the talking janitor (with dog breath).

There are other legendary cleaners, too, such as "Goldie the Ghost," who just floats silently through the area.

The rule that helps me figure out how to handle things here is the same one I was taught for shaking hands with a woman: "Let a woman offer her hand first if she wants to shake hands." So while I'm cleaning I smile and greet each person I come across briefly. If they initiate a conversation or ask a question, I've learned not to take this as an invitation to give them the inaugural speech of cleaning science. Answer briefly. If they pursue it further, I add a little to the time and subject but let them keep the initiative. Even if they pursue it too far, as long as you stay on your feet and in action, they'll soon say, "Well, I know you're working; I'll let you go."

You'll have to develop your own style to fit your situation and clients. I know that in schools with hundreds of precious little grade schoolers who all love the janitor, you'd never get a crumb picked up all day if you socialized to capacity. You need to stay super sensitive to this if you want to be a super professional.

You do want to exchange greetings with all you meet. I don't mean get carried away, make like you're running for governor and use up your days waving and shaking hands. But when you're passing through or move into an area to clean, **always acknowledge the people present**. Let them you know they're there.

It's a kind of tricky thing to get the greeting just right. Some cleaners are cold and lifeless, a body with no spirit, and some are overkill on the hoof, like a leech or lecher the public can't wait to get away from. Keeping in just the right lane here is important—know your bounds and stay in them.

One of the best ones is...

1. Thank you! Learn to say it to the people you clean for. Yes, I know they might not deserve it, and maybe they should be saying thanks to you. But this is the first step in teaching society we deserve more thanks. Start saying thanks yourself, in person and even with cards and notes. One time I thanked a tenant for cleaning up his area, and guess what? Not only did he keep his own place cleaner, he got all his buddies to do the same. They saved me tons of work, plus they treated me better and liked me more, too. All because of a tiny little note of thanks.

Don't be gushy, just alert for the opportunity when someone makes an effort to keep things clean or otherwise be helpful. Mention how it helped you and graciously say, "Thanks, I really appreciate what you did."

Mahalo! —That's thanks in Hawaiian.

2. Smile: Give them a big grin, a slight smile, or a flashy one, but smile as you pass.

3. Nod: Nod with a cordial look in your eye as you pass or enter. Or you can tip your hat to women.

4. Look at them, not your work, when you're talking to them. When someone asks you something, such as what are you doing or what are you using to clean, then turn your full attention on them and have the courtesy to answer. Look them in the eye and listen intently. They'll love you for it.

5. Wave (even with a paint brush or bowl brush); people like that.

6. Be cheerful (fake it if you have to).

7. "Please" is an even more magical word for cleaners than it is for children.

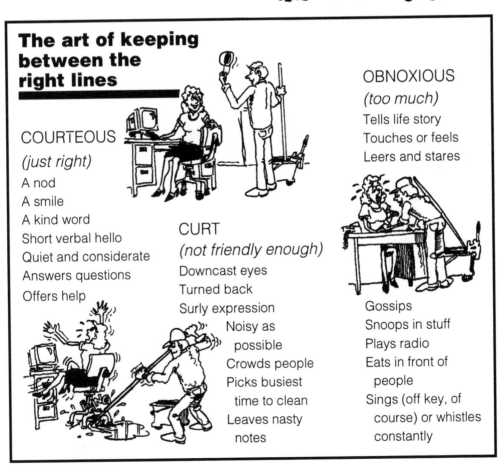

The art of keeping between the right lines

COURTEOUS
(just right)
A nod
A smile
A kind word
Short verbal hello
Quiet and considerate
Answers questions
Offers help

CURT
(not friendly enough)
Downcast eyes
Turned back
Surly expression
Noisy as
  possible
Crowds people
Picks busiest
  time to clean
Leaves nasty
  notes

OBNOXIOUS
(too much)
Tells life story
Touches or feels
Leers and stares

Gossips
Snoops in stuff
Plays radio
Eats in front of
  people
Sings (off key, of
  course) or whistles
  constantly

8. Learn to say **"May I?"**

9. Ask, "Would it bother you if I picked up/cleaned right here for a minute?" "Is this vacuum bothering you?"

10. Say **"Excuse me"** whenever you are moving through, in front of, or behind people.

11. Apologize if you missed or forgot something or somehow goofed. "Jumping germs, did I do that?"

12. Be willing. Learn to say "I'll be glad to." "Is there anything else I can do?"

Our Clients' Right to Privacy
(or what to do about what you see, hear, and find on the job)

There are some unmentioned but very real menaces in your position as a cleaner, and they have to do with personal privacy.

Face it, fellow cleaners, our job gives us unbelievable access to people's possessions and their personal privacy. If we're even half awake, we see, hear, and even handle the evidence of tens of thousands of other people's most private activities. All of which puts us in the most critical position of trust in the building.

This is a sensitive if not downright dangerous area.

True, some people seem to think we are fixtures or furnishings that don't comprehend what is going on. You and I know how wrong they are. We have emotions, temptations, and curiosity about other people's lives like anyone else. The fact that we are privileged to be right in the middle of things, however, means we have a truly sacred responsibility not to break faith with or injure our clients. One of the greatest compliments and assists to job security you can get as a cleaner is to gain the complete trust and respect of those you clean for or around. Here are some ways to accomplish that.

No matter how juicy the news (gossip) you come across might be, blabbing it all over the office, town, church, or bar—or for that matter to *anyone*—is going to get you and others into some sorry messes. It can make for ugly feelings and situations on the job! This is officially called confidentiality, meaning you are never going to be a communications center for people's personal lives. Good news or bad stays where you heard or saw it. Being discreet and silent takes some discipline, but to be a top cleaning person you have to develop this virtue. So far, we only have authority to clean people's premises, not their private lives; so don't tell anything, no matter how tempting (and it will be tempting).

☛ **The Golden Rule of Privacy:**
What you hear, see, or find
in a building, home, or room
you are cleaning *stays* in
that building, home, or room.

Stick to the right dirt!

Gossip is the world's favorite activity—even ahead of sex, sports, and eating, and wouldn't you know it, we janitors have the juiciest network in the neighborhood. We have temptation beyond imagining to pass it on or even add to it, fan the flames. **Don't do it, -0-, period, no, never, shame!** Even if it just kills you to keep it to yourself, forget it. Avoid listening to any of it and never spread it. A good janitor needs to have big ears, and big eyes too, and quick hands to perform excellent work, but a big mouth we don't need. Not only is a cleaning gossip lower than the scum they clean, but a blabbing janitor is hated by all.

☞ **Clean ON but not IN!** is always the rule, except when cleaning toilets or wastebaskets! I've made it a lifetime commitment never to look in anyone's drawers, desks, files, anything with a door or a lid on it. If it needs cleaning, I get permission first. People love it when you ask. It's a great courtesy and a great trouble preventer.
Clean well on, under, and over, but never IN personal storage.

☞ **Never look at, read, rubberneck,** or meddle in anything personal on desks, counters, tables, etc. Just clean and move on—and don't handle it except to clean it.

☞ **Going through wastebaskets** and garbage, when you see something valuable in there, is another no-no. I hate seeing things wasted, too, but nothing will lose you respect and jobs faster than having a client or the public see you raid-

ing the trash and fishing out something you figure someone else was stupid to pitch in. It takes time away from your job, and others who see you think it's equivalent to grave robbing and they will misinterpret it. In some cases where policy makes it permissible, such as with leftover food following a convention or banquet, make sure you *do* have permission and then be open about it.

☞ **Honor admittance restriction signs.** When a door says Authorized Personnel Only and you are allowed by policy, that means you only, and not a friend, relative, or **even a spouse**.

☞ **Invading an occupied room** is always poor taste, even if it needs cleaning, and especially if you crane your neck and work more slowly as you sweep or vacuum by the center of things. If you barge into a place that should be empty and isn't, say loudly, "Excuse me, I'll clean this later," and back out quietly. They'll love your sensitivity!

☞ **Lingering and stalling around** something that doesn't concern you is a bad thing to do. When something interesting is going on and you edge closer or drift

69

over and dust for two hours on one desktop, it really looks bad for you and the cleaning industry. Don't stop and listen to a conversation or event that doesn't concern you. It will be tempting at times just for curiosity's sake, but don't do it, even if it's right in your path. Don't eavesdrop, never repeat, and walk (or even run) away from conversations that are definitely none of your business.

☞ **Asking questions about personal things**—habits, romances, official or business matters, politics, finances—is a gross invasion of privacy. Something like "Wow, Mr. Jones, this a nice office! You must be rich. How much do you make?" is as crude as can be.

☞ **Getting involved.** Every place we work, cleaning homes, commercial build-

ings, or tending landscaping, there are "real life soap opera" episodes going on. Many are powder kegs. If you arrive somewhere or just happen to be there cleaning when a heated discussion or an argument is in progress, or when romantic words and emotions are at large, move away immediately. People may do things like this around us, thinking we are deaf and dumb or can't understand. We can, but don't get involved. Move on.

Often people may not know you're around the corner or in the next stall cleaning and will reveal some secret side of their job or life, from drugs to rum running (I actually had a gun runner working with me once, 20 years ago). Again here you didn't ask for it, but you got it. It's like a hot coal—you better handle it right or you'll burn yourself and the rest of the place down.

We cleaning people have a way of working our way into the hearts and lives of others, and since we always seem to be around, people will often unload some very private and personal matters on us. Things we really shouldn't hear or know, but we do.

One answer to this is to fake embarrassment when someone starts into a vivid description of a family fight, a recent surgery, or his drinking problem.

If you get into a pattern of listening to personal problems, politics, love life, financial struggles, etc., you'll end up in more trouble than they have. Just adding your "2 cents' worth" can cost you a bunch of time and grief, or even your job. Many good cleaners in good-

paying jobs and positions have been dismissed because of involvement or interference in the personal matters of clients or other employees. In short, we need to concentrate on the soap solution at work and not the soap opera.

True, as human beings we are there to help, but as cleaning professionals our primary objective is to care for and clean up the building, not everyone's social and emotional ills. We may sometimes get pulled into the net of noncleaning problems, find the company accountant weeping in the janitor closet or the boss drunk in the boiler room. In cases like this we have no choice but to respond, but respond by leading or directing the injured party to proper authorities and channels. Refer or take them to the personnel department, a supervisor, or the company doctor or nurse. Carry their crying towel, but not their heartache. "Can I help you?" is something we always want to ask, but let's not confuse help with doing things or dabbling into situations we should stay out of.

☛ **Keep your hands to yourself.** Shaking hands is about the only touching of people that is in order in the cleaning life. Be extra aware of this as a cleaner. You might feel the urge to squeeze an arm, pat a back, pinch a cheek (or something else)... **don't do it**. Little or big, old or young, don't do it. Ninety percent of people will be really offended.

Compassion can all too easily turn to passion, and even innocent involvement can get you charged with meddling or molesting. Never touch, hug, etc. anyone while at work. Shake hands or salute, help, lead, talk, smile, serve, but keep your heart and hands to yourself. This goes for your dealings with fellow cleaners as well as clients. This is a day of lawsuits, even for intentions. Don't give anyone the opportunity to misjudge you. Avoid physical contact at all times.

☛ **Creeping up on people.** Some of you might like to be reborn as a cougar or an Indian scout, because you love to creep up on people and scare them out of their senses. The better you get at it, the softer-soled shoes you buy. It might be fun for you and a kick to talk about in the janitor closet with the gang, but it's pretty uncouth to walk up on and startle someone who doesn't even know you're around. This kind of surprise is just another invasion of privacy. Don't do it. If you walk unnoticed into a room or an area or come up behind someone's back, clear your throat, snort, whistle one bar, tap the door, tap dance, rattle the bucket, or come out with a polite "Excuse me"—one way or another make your presence known.

71

☞ Beware of the **biggest myth** of cleaning: Thinking that no one sees you because you are the only one in the building. Even if it's 2 a.m. and yours is the only car in the lot, this is **wrong, wrong, wrong**. Somehow, some way, your actions on the job are always known. Everyone eventually finds out where you were and what you were doing. You may think it's a mystery, but in these days of security cameras and two-way mirrors, it's not so hard to figure out. Always be alert and keep on doing what you're supposed to be doing.

Handling complaints

"Complaint" is a familiar tune to janitors, and never music to our ears. Reading and following this book will cut your complaints in half, I promise, but there are some people who won't be satisfied even if you clean their toilets with a golden swab. People will always expect the positive and report the negative. No matter how well or consistently you clean, customers and clients will gradually just expect it and say nothing. But when an occasional problem arises, they come to life—screaming, threatening, and even bullying you.

Handling any complaint, justified or unjustified, in a positive way will be a big plus for you. Anyone, by complaining, is finally giving you some attention, that's great. Now make it positive, and it takes only 4 simple steps.

1. Listen! Just look at them and listen and let them lay the whole load on you. Then when they run down, ask for more. Get it all out, don't defend or excuse anything or anyone. Just listen.

2. Cry with them. Express sorrow, concern, pity, understanding. Reinforce their reasons, feel worse about it than they do. "You poor woman, an unemptied wastebasket for two whole days! Gasp! How did you get by?" (They now know you heard them and share their concern.)

3. Take it off them. Take the problem away, even just to assign it to someone else, instead of sending *them* somewhere to do something about it. Get the details of what they want and when, and then you go take care of it or do it.

4. DO MORE. Most people with a problem have a remedy or a repayment they expect to make things right. Generally it is pretty fair—but always give them a little more than they ask for, kind of a recompense for their having been put out. Make it better than they expect—they will forget the complaint and **never** forget you.

Finding favor... not favors

The longer you have a job, the better you get at it, and the wider range of responsibilities you assume, the more people will know and depend on you. This is a great goal to achieve as a professional cleaner—unless we allow ourselves to become used rather than useful. I've seen many sincere cleaners work themselves into this particular hangman's noose.

Example: Fred cleans a grade school during the week and a church on Saturdays—48 hours of cleaning a week. He loves the jobs and earns a good living. Always eager to serve, he breaks his butt to do everything he's asked to do and more. Seeing this, the people he cleans around start to add little non-janitor jobs like starting their cars when it's 30° below, picking up the mail, watering and fertilizing the houseplants. Or maybe just letting them borrow, take home, the school's or church's equipment and tools for personal use. Fred, like many custodians, can

do almost anything, and soon they have him repairing lamps and fixing typewriters. As they give him more and more to do, Fred comes in earlier and stays later; soon he's doing literally dozens of non-cleaning jobs. They praise him to the sky, but slowly it becomes clear that all his time (which the state and church were paying for) is going to serve a few individuals, a minister and three teachers. There isn't much time left to get his work done. His boss chews him out. When Fred cuts back his extra favors, the clients become angry with him, call him lazy, and complain to his boss (to get even with their loss of an errand boy). Finally after suffering unmercifully, Fred, an honest and caring professional, loses his job.

This is a fine line and a deadly one. We need to be willing to help and do extra when and if we can, but without ever forgetting what our basic duties are. It takes tact and wisdom to juggle this. It helps to remember that if a hundred people in a building each ask for only five extra minutes of your time for their personal non-work related jobs, that's eight hours. There goes your day!

People will not only ask you for extras, they'll sometimes offer extras to you. Gifts, tokens, tips, prizes, bribes—you'll be amazed at some of the little things clients will come up with. If you know what to watch out for and how to deal with the potential traps, both you and your company will benefit.

1. Errands: Only in emergencies, not on a regular basis. Politely explain that you have a schedule to keep.

2. Salespeople: Most are honest, but be cautious about taking incentives and prizes like radios and jackets for orders. Before you know it you are beholden to them and their products.

3. Gifts: A hat, T-shirt, pencil, or key chain may be okay (check your company policy), but cash, appliances, prizes, etc. are suicide, just like those college athletics payoffs.

4. Personal cleaning jobs: Here's a real judgment call. You may do something once to show them how, but let them know you have rules to follow and you can't be sidetracked from your job. If it gets touchy, recommend they clear it with your supervisor.

5. Loaning company equipment for a personal job: Never do it.

CHAPTER 5

WATCH YOUR STEP HERE:
Staying Out of Hot Water

The Fine Line Between Fun and Fooling Around

Nothing is better than having a good time on the job, really enjoying what you do and who you are working with. And yes, even in the cleaning crew we have our comedians (or commodians), artists, pranketeers, singers, athletes—all doing their thing to entertain and keep away the sometimes perceived boredom of cleaning. GREAT! Let's let the public know we are human and can laugh and play as well as anyone. However… let's have some class and be more dignified than the others!

(Horseplay… can give us a kick in the head)

Nobody wants to see a janitor with a sour face or a grumpy attitude. When you're alive, enthusiastic, vibrant, humorous, and even capable of a joke or two… more power to you. Personality helps keep things clean. A little good-natured interplay with each other when we're working, and even with the customers (careful here) is great. However—and this is crucial—it has to be in good taste. You were hired for your horsepower and horse sense, not for horseplay. So think before scuffling or roughhousing, pulling stunts or gags that might backfire or injure someone, notes that could be read by others than those intended, etc.

Here are a few biggies to be aware of:

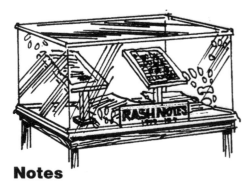

Notes

Bad ones make excellent evidence against you. If you ever write one that contains any crudeness or anger, criticism or profanity, I promise you it will be preserved and pulled forth forever to haunt you. Keep any written correspondence with clients or *anyone* cordial, positive, unjudgmental, and free of anger and threats of any kind, and you'll keep your job and your self-respect.

Tricks and Gags

We've all booby trapped something sometime, stacked up the janitor closet or put rubber dog poop in the toilet to get a reaction out of the rest of the crew. Keep any little tricks positive and loving and strictly for a laugh. Always ask yourself first: Is this safe, physically and emotionally, for others and for me?

Scuffles

More often than I'd like to admit, I've seen full-grown men suddenly acting like two competing bulls in spring—start (usually good naturedly) slapping and cuffing and pushing each other. If the urge for a little wrestling is overwhelming, go to the exercise room or out on the lawn. Slips and falls while fooling around can cost you pain and heartbreak and the boss a lot of liability. And especially inside a building, even the slightest move interpreted as aggressive stabs observing do-gooders to the very heart.

Equipment and Machinery

Use it only as intended. Races with janitor carts, jousting or swordfighting with mops (I'm giving you all kinds of ideas, right?), dueling with spray bottles filled with cleaning chemicals, playing flying saucer with buffer pads, etc., is exhilarating and does break up the day a little, but it will also break up the building, desks, fixtures, etc. If you're going to do things like this, do them away from work, outside, or in an organized way at the next company picnic.

Janitor damage

We see others beating up our building—tenants breaking, stealing, and spilling things, leaning chairs and feet against the wall, knocking holes in things... and we cleaners get pretty huffy.

What if I told you that you and the cleaners of the world—including me—do more damage to any building than the users?
We do!

Let me give you a down home example, the restroom. Now how can secretaries, executives, or any office worker ruin a toilet or sink or floor using it? They may leave *Wall Street Journals* or *Woman's Day* or other messes around, but (except for the occasional vandalism, scribble on the stall wall, or sanitary napkin accidentally flushed down the toilet) actual damage seldom occurs. Now enter Ronald Ruin, the custodian. He uses acid in there all the time and drips and splashes it on the chrome, etching it permanently and turning it green. He stands on the toilet seat (and wrecks it) reaching up to clean.

He sands the shine off ceramic tile using flint-hard powdered cleansers and abrasive pads (the wrong ones). He drops things on the tile and chips it, leans mops against the walls and marks them, props doors open with broom handles—wrenching the door and marking the handle. His cart scrapes the stall and door casings going in and out, he pokes a hole in the tile ceiling while rinsing the mop in the bucket, lays a cigarette on top of the dispenser while working and burns it... Need I go on? The other day, walking through a beautiful 30-story building barely two years old, it was easy to see that 99 percent of the nicks, scrapes, holes, and other damage could easily be linked to the cleaning people, their carts, vacuums with the bumper guards off, and so on. All of the doors were scarred on both sides from floor tools. The damage was pitiful and would take about $100,000 to restore it to new—and it was all caused by cleaning.

This is serious, and bosses and owners are very aware of it and get very uptight about it. We ought to be fired on the spot for hurting a building and speeding up its depreciation. Here are some guidelines to help you stay "Not Guilty."

- Have bumper guards on vacuums and all floor tools 100% of the time—no exceptions.

- Work with splash guards on floor machines to avoid unnecessary splashing of walls, furniture, and baseboards. Never allow the handle or body of the machine to strike against walls, furniture, or equipment.

- Never lean or stack anything against any wall anywhere, anytime.

- Don't use mop buckets and carts as battering rams to push open doors.

- Never prop open doors with equipment or tool handles. Use rubber wedges only.

- Reckless moving of scaffolds inside a building beats up walls, doors, and door frames (and can knock things off desks, etc.). Get someone to help!

- Eliminate powdered cleansers and other abrasive cleaners, bleach, and chemicals that do damage from your cleaning arsenal.

- Never yank electric cords or plugs sideways.

- Never set anything that belongs on the floor on a desk or other furnishing.

- Include an anti-damage session in all training programs to keep everyone aware of this subject.

- Keep furniture you move in hand. Never slide, skid, or skate it.

- Don't drag—lift (with help if necessary) anything heavy across the floor, whether it's vinyl, tile, cement, or carpet.

- Never use equipment (like mop buckets, buffers, etc.) to block or detour a walkway. Use the standard yellow cones or signs.

Family and friends on the job

You love them, and they may be smart and good looking, as well as honest, upstanding, brave, clean, and reverent. But bringing your family and friends on or around the job is generally not a good idea. The vast majority of the people you work for, even those who love children and have six kids themselves, will be offended if you bring your own children on the cleaning job with you. Or even have a family member sit there and read quietly while you work—or worse yet, have them help you. When someone is not officially hired, the liability risks for safety and security are so great that your boss or management is bound to be uptight and irritated. And this only leads to negative feelings about you. **Bringing buddies along to help,** even if they aren't getting paid, is out of line, no matter how right it may seem to you. The rule in professional cleaning is that if they don't work in the building as a regular scheduled crew member, then they shouldn't be there.

This may seem a little harsh, but trust me, it isn't. It only makes good sense for all of us. Here are some good reasons why from my own company's experience.

One little six-year-old, for instance, got tangled in some stage ropes while his father was cleaning, and almost strangled himself. Other children have started fires or pushed the Fire button while playing and panicked half the town. Things like having water fights or playing hide-and-seek in the lobby may seem innocent enough, but they can cause damage and injury, too. Older children and teens will often use the clients' phones (they love those 900 numbers!) or entertain themselves with the copier. And more "friends" than you would imagine (who don't feel the loy-

alty to the company that you do) will come into the building with you and steal things. Or slip and fall on something, get into fights, or get lost (so that you have to get security to find them).

Even if they don't pose any threat to themselves or their surroundings, we can be sure that the presence of our loved ones will do nothing for our concentration on the job at hand. We can't give what we're doing our full attention when 80 percent of our brain cells are occupied with where the baby is wandering now or what sister Sue is saying.

I'm not talking about when long-lost friends or your folks or grandfolks come through town and you ask them to come by the workplace for a few minutes to meet the boss and see where you work. These are "guests" and bosses like guests. But they don't like a spouse or friend showing up early to pick you up and then tapping their fingers or pacing around in the lobby or in the hall, as you hustle to get that final job done. Or parking right outside the back door or otherwise in the way, revving their motor and honking, as if you are sinning to finish your shift. Guests are welcome, but regular hangers-on or hangers-out will hang you!

Many bosses, likewise, are besieged by mothers and fathers who can't let their kids alone on a new job—they have to call several times a week to check on things and evaluate them. If you have overprotective parents, ask them to cool it! Concern is okay; direct contact with your employer over YOUR job isn't, except maybe in an emergency.

While we're on this subject, bear in mind that you usually don't have the right to extend company privileges such as permits, passes, rides, and dorm rooms to personal friends. Asking a friend to ride along with you en route to somewhere or when you're delivering something somewhere in a company vehicle is totally taboo, even if you have six empty seats. Too much freedom with company fringes is a quick way to court suspicion or suspension from your boss.

You can't hide these things, either. You

take the kids along in a emergency once and nothing bad happens, so you're tempted to do it again, and then again, and then regularly, and then... something always happens. Many an executive has come in some morning and found animal cracker crumbs on the seat of his leather chair, where your two-year-old left them. When that sooner or later something does happen because unauthorized people were in the building, who will have to answer for it? You. And when you're called in to answer for it, you may not even have been aware that your buddy or girl or boy friend who came to work with you was tying up the phone or using the computer. You'll be sick, and your job situation will be even sicker.

This is an easy one to cure. Just make a firm rule—no family or friends on the job with you. Then make it known to everyone and make no exceptions.

P.S. This goes for your furry family, too For similar reasons, you never want to bring your pets to work with you either. You have enough to do there without worrying about which pile of papers they'll decide to play with, whether they'll remember their potty training, and where did your pet boa constrictor slither to.

Family and friends on the payroll

Another "too close for comfort" caution is that thing called nepotism. Often a family member, close friend, neighbor, or club acquaintance will go to work with or around you, whether or not you hired them.

This is a fuse you must be careful never to light or it will explode. No matter how fairly you might deal with family or how hard and well they work, everyone else will see it as favoring them or catering to them with easy jobs or schedules. Things like this cause an amazing number of problems in cleaning activities. If family wants your job someday or wants to go to work in the same department, run it through another channel and let them handle it. And anticipate the coming prejudice and criticism—it will come. It's great to work with and around family and friends, and to help people out with jobs, but be advised that cleaning history shows this situation has plenty of sharp edges you need to keep turned in.

Your own personal problems

Keep them to yourself. At work, your love life, health, finances, and for that matter any aspects of your strictly personal being don't need to be broadcast around or announced to clients or fellow cleaners. We both know they have plenty of problems of their own—they don't need any more unloaded on them. And no

matter how much they may like us personally, the first concern of those who employ us is 1. will we show up and keep on showing up? and 2. will we do a good job? Personal problems, the ones we can't help as well as the ones we cause, are only a threat to these bottom line concerns.

Pursuing personal business on company time

I know it isn't always easy to separate personal things from work, but every boss is jealous of your time when s/he's paying for it. Bringing books to read, taking personal calls, spending hours discussing personal problems or upcoming social events is really a dishonest thing to do. A few occasional or emergency things, taking a note or two or making a quick call to order furnace oil or a Valentine delivery is okay. But too many cleaners think that when things get slow they should start in on some of their personal projects on company time. Spending an hour like that is exactly like stealing one hour's worth of wages, taking $10, from your boss's dresser drawer. If you ask permission first, doing some special thing once in a great while is okay, but when you get right down to it, pursuing any kind of personal project during work

hours is off limits to a real pro.

That goes for soliciting contributions, selling tickets or Girl Scout cookies, distributing merchandise or publications, etc. This really burns up the management and has a bad effect on your fellow cleaners, who say to themselves, if your church or pyramid sales group can do it, we can do it too. Imagine if all 16 people in one office start doing this—you have a big-time problem!

Your paycheck: Keep it private

Your salary or rates and raises and what kind of deal you have with your clients and bosses should always be kept strictly to yourself, for your own benefit and that of others. When you broadcast your pay scale to all, you limit flexibility for yourself and others. I had a super worker, for example, getting paid the same as everyone else, though he deserved more. I slipped him a $300 bonus one month and he ran out and blabbed to all his fellow workers. They didn't deserve a cent more than they were making, but now they all hated him and were all mad at me, so now I couldn't slip the guy any more bonuses. Keep your financial deals private, from both the public and your buddies.

Your criticisms, too

Negative opinions and appraisals of the boss, the supervisors, the company, your coworkers your pay, your schedule, your equipment, are all death to your job. Even if these opinions are accurate, remember that criticism can get a soldier the firing squad and get you fired. You gain nothing from criticizing and expressing your opinion out loud, in public, about things that displease you. Swallow the urge and let it pass, or talk about it in private to your supervisor or boss. Or even quit if things are too bad, but **don't complain out loud**. This means expressions and gestures too—raised eyebrows, crafty chuckles, and snarls say "non-support" just as clearly to the hand that feeds you.

Know your place

It's always in good taste to KNOW YOUR PLACE. It's not in the gutter or locked in the closet, but we, like the construction worker, the disc jockey, and the chef, do have "our place" of work. We aren't necessarily servants, but we are in a service business and we have to be careful about the way we mix with the other people in commercial buildings or homes while on the job. For example, one evening you take your best friend to a fancy, high-priced restaurant for the big dinner of the year. Right when you are mid-meal, four of the cooks barge out of the kitchen in their greasy cooking garb and sit down at the table next to you where they eat and laugh and carry on. It would offend you and others. It's not that the cooks aren't as good as you or anyone else or that they don't deserve to eat, but their place **while working** isn't in the dining room with the customers.

If a business executive came and hung out in your janitor closet you wouldn't like it either, so be cautious where and when and with whom you take breaks. Another time I was cleaning a big church, and one of my cleaners was an accomplished pianist. Right in his paint clothes, he jumped off the ladder and began playing the grand piano. That deeply offended the owners of the building, and I can understand why. He may not have been hurting it, but the piano was private property and not for off-the-cuff worker creativity. If he'd asked and played his solo afterwards or at the next Sunday service, it would have been fine, but during work it was bad PR! I've seen clients get really angry when janitors or maids help themselves to goodies on the table of a convention or dinner party where they happen to be working. They don't mind the guests and public eating, but for the cleaning people to amble by and snatch morsels from the tray is offensive.

The importance of showing up!!

A few years ago, there was a flood in New Orleans, and the world stopped to read the disaster story. Everything was cut off—traffic, electricity, phones, etc., and the whole city ground to a halt... except for one faithful janitor who had never missed a day of work. He walked, waded, and swam fifteen miles through cottonmouth-infested water, and he made it to the building he was entrusted with the care of... on **time**! Now there is a real hero, and one of us, too!

"Absence makes the heart grow fonder" may be true, but it usually means fonder of someone else. That's the way it is, especially in a job situation. When you aren't there, people may honor your excuses and adjust, but the wheels of alternative or replacement are already turning. Some people can miss work, have their calls re-routed, their territory temporarily handled by someone else, their meetings rescheduled—they may hardly be missed. But there's a lot of difference between office paper and toilet paper. Run out of both and see which one gets the most attention! Being gone is always negative, even when you're "entitled" to

be gone. Taking sick leave, for example, when you aren't sick isn't ethical. These aren't days you have coming and can miss any old time at the expense of the company.

We cleaning people do have one of the best records of attendance, some of the best marks for showing up to work, but we need to better them. If you really want to be secure, valued and kept around in your job, if you want to get raises and promotions, etc., about the smartest move you can make is to **be there every single day you're supposed to be**. I know people who haven't missed work in more than thirty years, and they're the real heroes in my book. Those who are always cutting time off the front and back and middle of their shift are slowly cutting themselves out of a job. So:

1. Be there... even if it's tough at times.

2. In an emergency, **worry about your replacement,** even if it's technically your supervisor's worry. Help and search and suggest and do whatever you can to make sure your area is covered, your work done, and your customers taken care of properly.

3. Be on time—no—**be a little early.** Early gives your boss and your fellow workers confidence in you, gives you leadership and respect. Early is ambitious, early feels good, and early covers some of those little slip-ups, too.

4. Give a little extra. Beating the quitting whistle by five minutes beats you out of many subtle advantages. Start giving five minutes every day instead of taking it, and watch how much better things turn out for you.

Will all this go unnoticed? *Never!* Often we think our faithful attendance and extra time and effort go unnoticed by the big boss. Don't be fooled; most bosses got where they are through rigid attention to attendance and plenty of extra hours, so they do notice and will eventually reward you. So will everyone else.

Some of us punch a clock, but most of us are on the honor system when it comes to our comings and goings, breaks and lunchtimes. A word to the wise here is to give more than you take. On time is good, early is great! Did you ever stop to think that there's usually only about 5-8 minutes of difference between the person who leaves work first and the one who leaves last—and think of all the respect the boss has for that "last" leaver!!

Some off-the-job action that can help (or hurt) a professional cleaner

"What I do on my own time and in my own home and in my own private life is my own business."

I've heard this plenty of times and so have you. We probably both agree with it 100 percent. But I would like to give you some additional thoughts to add to this seeming truism of personal rights and freedoms.

Whatever profession you're in, like it or not, it follows you everywhere, every minute. An architect or a plumber is still an architect or plumber on a hunting trip, at his daughter's wedding, or playing with his grandkids. The realm of your job is yours; you wear it like a cloak. Trying to forget what you do for a living when you're off work is like trying to forget you're married when you're away from home. People will ask you questions about your cleaning profession, talk with you about it, come by the house to borrow your cleaning gear, and even ask you to help. The committee will turn to you for cleanup assignments. Some people really fight this as an invasion of their personal lives, but I totally disagree. You don't leave teachings and commitments behind once church is over, nor can or should you run away from your profession. Why not enhance it in your off hours? It'll make it that much better when you're back on the job. (See p. 88.)

One little caution now. There is a gray area to be careful of here, and it's called Conflict of Interest! Some people, for example, are on the cleaning staff at the factory or the plant or the office, and they also have their own cleaning business. There's a fine line to be aware of here ethically. It's a good idea to capitalize on what you know, but on the other hand, I know of good building managers who got involved with other cleaning companies and were accused of trading favors, favoritism, and using company cleaning contacts for their personal advantage. This can get pretty touchy, so watch out for it.

CHAPTER 6

CURES FOR THE JOB BLAHS AND BLUES (When You're Not Loving Every Minute of it)

Are you ashamed to admit... "I clean"?

I never could understand how anyone could be ashamed of doing honest work, especially clean, honest work. While doing some cleaning consulting work in New York City, I was told that some cleaners would sue the company if the true nature of their jobs were revealed to the public. "Naw," I said, "how could that be?" "Oh, yes. For example, Harry and his wife work in a 33-story building cleaning restrooms, and they each make $28,000 a year (a joint income of $56,000 a year back in 1978 was very good—nothing to sneeze at). They live in upstate New York, and when the day is over, they change into sport clothes, get into their Cadillac, and drive home. It's important to them that their neighbors not know what they do, so we've been advised by their attor-

neys not to reveal the fact that they're cleaners."

Pretty silly. One of Harry's neighbors was probably a proctologist (who spends his days looking up people's hind ends) and another a dentist (works in enamel just like Harry, only in someone's mouth, bathed in spit and horsebreath).

What is class?

Too many people connect it with a job, title, position, location, or way of dressing. It doesn't actually have much to do with any of those things. A janitor with integrity, ambition, commitment, and true devotion to the building and the people it serves is an undisputed class act that few can match or challenge. Class comes from classy conduct—good attitude and sincere effort. People who learn their job and do it well and willingly are **first class... period!**

Never be ashamed of what you do, if you do it well. No job on earth has higher class or has more worthwhile results than "clean."

Family disfavor? Hold your head high

Nearly any job will draw criticism from family and friends. And let's face it, fellow cleaners, lots and lots of people—if not all of them—deep in their hearts, think cleaning is a demeaning job. Close friends may be polite enough not to say anything, but they'll probably still think it. I say that's their problem, not yours. If you let it get to you, however, it will be your problem.

Even if you're fulfilled and happy in your work, if people close to you are critical of your profession, it can create

misery. Your spouse may like the money but not the job. You may overhear, "Oh I wish my husband would do something else." Or you may be hurt that Junior never shows you off on career day. You may endure it, but it's still a nerve-grating thing to pack around or have tucked in the back of your mind.

We have three choices here:

1. Change jobs

2. Put up with it

3. Change public opinion

If you like your job and the boss likes you, that eliminates #1. And we're all tired of #2. So let's go for Number 3, and change others' view of us or help them change it themselves. Here's how:

Educate

Yes, that word that solves so many problems is a cleaning professional's best friend. Sit down and tell people about your job. Educate them about what you actually do, why it's worthwhile, and why you love it. You'll be surprised how many people have no idea what a job in the cleaning field entails.

Tell them about the profession, the tools, the chemicals, and your importance to the building, the people who use it, and the environment. You'll be amazed how a little knowledge opens minds. Even take them to a building you clean (with permission) to show them your skills and the pride and trust you have. It will blow them away and the stigma against cleaning, too.

Talk

Talk openly to everyone about the exciting things you do, see, and experience on the job. Go ahead and brag about all you learn, the exercise you get, the great people you meet, the lives you change, the friends you have in your cleaning associates and your clients. Sit down someday and make a list of the good things you get from your job, and you won't have to carry it with you after that to remember the pluses. A cleaner seldom brags about his or her job; mostly they remain silent while the policemen, secretaries, or sales managers talk it up. Our profession is much more exciting, and it doesn't take long to make people jealous that they aren't cleaners.

Live it

Live your cleaning religion. If you're a pro cleaner, then make the profession part of your everyday life. This, too, will show people that cleaning is the biggest and best profession in the world—it offers stimulation, education, excitement, self-development, and good pay. WHY should you live your cleaning religion?

Everywhere you go—work, play, home, and church—people will know what you do. If they sense that you know and love your job, they'll become interested in, if not downright enthusiastic about, it too. Once that happens they'll respect you, help you, boost you, and promote you, and life will improve both at work and at home.

We've all heard many times, "Well, I leave my job at work" but why do that? If you're a veterinarian, mechanic, or photographer, you're still one at dinner, a ball game, a concert, or a family reunion. You don't quit being what you are when the time or location changes. If one of the pack animals is injured on a camping trip, the jeep won't start, or the group is posing, a real professional doesn't say, "Oh, I left that skill at work." A professional is a professional always and everywhere. And so a cleaner is a cleaner, every minute of his or her life, whether being paid at the time or not. So anytime your skills are needed or there's an opportunity to talk or learn more about them is the right time to claim your identity. By your words and actions, proclaim the reasons cleaning makes you and others—the world—better and happier.

It enhances your job to live it all the time, just as it enhances your religious beliefs to live them. No one likes "Sunday Christians" (folks who claim allegiance to a moral standard or philosophy but never practice it the other days of the week). Our religion is "clean," and we don't just do it for a living! We don't want to be on-the-job cleaners only; that's dull and limiting. The real fun of life is doing things, well and often, using our talents and spirit to help, teach, and strengthen others. People say to me, "Boy, you sure like what you do, Don!" and I do. So I've lived my profession every day, on and off the job, for more than thirty years now.

Like you, I've been through many long tiring bouts of cleaning at 3 a.m., being unappreciated, cleaning poop off bathroom walls, being accused of snitching a few dried-up cinnamon bears from a secretary's desk…. But I didn't just get discouraged about it—I took all of the thoughts and ideas it gave me and wrote them down. I also collected cleaning jokes and techniques, recorded the notable and funny happenings of the week, and took pictures. Then I started writing articles and little news stories for the company. I did all I could to dramatize and expand and build on what I was doing. I'm no photographer or newsman, but I did it anyway.

Then I began teaching people, showing them what I knew and what I learned. As you know, they are interested—people ask questions about what we do all the time. I gave little cleaning seminars free to home ec classes, church groups, and PTAs. Soon crowds of 100, 200, even 800 came to listen to the JANITOR and learn how to clean better. I put the information that was asked for most often into a pamphlet and sold it for a dollar—and people clawed to get it. I was no English major or writer, but like you I did know cleaning, so I expanded it into a book and called it *Is There Life After Housework?* Nobody would publish it, so I borrowed $30,000 (mighty hard to do as a janitor) and self-published it. I sold 20,000 copies right off, which in self-published books—especially about toilet cleaning—was unheard of. I finally got the attention of a national publisher, Writer's Digest, and went on to sell over a million books with them. I've written more than twenty books now with different publishers, all on cleaning, and they've sold over 2 million copies to date! They've been published in many different countries and languages, and I've appeared on TV and radio programs across the country and around the world to discuss cleaning. I've traveled to Europe, Canada, and Australia preaching the gospel of clean. And today I've expanded my cleaning job (besides books, articles, and my 15-state contract cleaning business) into one of the best libraries of cleaning information in the world, the largest Cleaning Museum, a mail order/retail store that makes professional tools and supplies available to homemakers, and a consulting service on maintenance-free design. Plus I'm working on at least 30 new book projects, *all related to cleaning.*

HOW to live your religion of clean

You don't need to wear a uniform and carry a wet floor sign to the PTA meeting or take it to bed with you. Just seize any opportunity to proclaim and boost your job, your chosen profession to others, especially outsiders. You'll not only benefit but enjoy life more if you do.

To give you some ideas, let me share some things I do.

Keep your own house clean! The big number one, of course, is keeping your own home, room, desk, car, yard, field,

front page of the paper and the caption mentions where you work, he'll love you for it.

Represent your profession to the community, just like the doctors and lawyers. Your profession is larger and older than either of theirs. You can run for the Senate or the school board, run the Little League, 4-H chapter, or Jr. Miss Pageant. I meet thousands of cleaners who think that because they're cleaners they're somehow not worthy or don't have a right to occupy key community positions. Nonsense. You are actually among the best qualified. Go for it. (Think of the slogans you could have in politics, "Mop up the opponent," "Flush out the crooks.")

equipment, purse, wallet, closet, etc. clean and neat all the time. If you believe in clean and you're getting paid to clean up after others, shouldn't your own domain be an example for all to see? Keeping your own house in order is the big, big number one to get you off to the right start of living your religion of clean. It takes only minutes to wash the car, vacuum it (and the trunk), clean off your desk at night, or straighten your shop. Be neat and life will be neater.

Volunteer for cleanup duty at parties, camp, community or church activities, and rally others to do so, too. It usually ends up more fun than the activity.

Offer to head up the anti-litter campaign or environmental program in your community. This will benefit everyone and be a real pleasure for you (a chance to put your skills to work for an important cause). And it'll really enhance your job. When your boss sees your picture on the

Be a walking source of cleaning know-how for neighbors, groups of any kind, schools. I carry cleaning novelties and information with me, and I'm always ready to jump in and hand them out and teach the kiddies.

How about teaching school assemblies about cleaning in your town? If you do it right, the kids will get a kick out of it and the mothers will mob you afterward for convincing those untidy little rascals to get with it.

Give cleaning classes. I teach cleaning at clubs, schools, companies, and meetings of all kinds, and people cheer (and I even get paid sometimes).

Collect stories. Cleaners end up in more funny situations than you can imagine. Write them down and spread them around. Everybody loves to laugh.

Subscribe to, read, and clip quotes, jokes, and wisdom from magazines and other publications in the cleaning field, and share them.

Start your own cleaning library. Collect books, articles, videos—all kinds of educational and reference material on cleaning—for your own use and that of others. Education enhances lives.

Give cleaning gifts. Need a gift for a wedding, shower, anniversary? There's no better, more practical present than a loaded maid's basket, one of my books, or a gift certificate for cleaning service!

Media! TV, radio, print—all want good, helpful information and what's better than solid, useful information about housecleaning or keeping the environment clean and litter free. You are the expert.

Write and sell articles, essays, stories, or poems about cleaning and maintenance. Submit them to newsletters, newspapers, magazines, and contests.

There's no magic involved here. Just be alert every day—look, listen, and collect thoughts and ideas while cleaning those toilet stalls, walls, and floors. Sometimes we're so focused on the immediate daily demands of the job that we don't realize the place we work and clean, and the people all around us, are just dripping with brilliant ideas, opportunities, and stories, which you can grab and digest and use.

Show your knowledge and pride in cleaning history. I have a full-fledged Cleaning Museum (undoubtedly the world's largest!), and anytime I travel anywhere, I look for things to add to it.

Invent! Sure! Who knows better than you what is needed to clean faster, better, and more economically? You can change lives and might even make money. See p. 58.

Make up attractive, tasteful **personalized stationery or business cards** that identify you as an expert in your field. It'll help insure that people treat you that way.

My tie is clipped with a **squeegee tie pin.** It stimulates many questions about what I do for a living.

A buffer clock! Why not? It tells time and tells everyone I'm a member of the world's largest profession—cleaning.

Have a buffer mailbox at home. Now that's class, and all who see it grin and nod and know I love my job and this helps me do it better.

A toilet plunger key chain? Oh yes, and it brings smiles and stories out of people you wouldn't believe. And if it's lost, everyone knows who it belongs to!

Toilet earrings. Nope, I'm not kidding. Proud cleaners wear them, to the delight of everyone. Puts our profession right up there with the crown jewels.

A toilet bouquet, why not? These clever little planters make it clear that a clean toilet is bright and cheery, and that you care!

Toilet soup or hot chocolate mug leaves no doubt at break time as to who you are and what you do for a living.

Chocolate outhouse! These make a fun housewarming gift or reward for the kid who finally cleans his room.

A squirting toilet. I carry one and I've even squirted governors, principals, and movie stars with it. Fun, but also helps people realize that professional cleaners are people!

Carry a **Johnny Lip Light** (little toilet inspection light) around with you and playfully scare people with the idea that you're going to use it. "I'm as good as any dentist (we both work in enamels!)."

Where do I find all this? I just keep my eyes and ears open; ideas are all over! With my constant use and flourishing of cleaning things, I can be the life of the party while helping to raise the visibility of our profession.

☛ For a free catalog of all these cleaning novelties and more, write to Cleaning Profession Catalog, PO Box 700, Pocatello, ID 83204.

When someone on the job (at any level) is making you miserable...

We finally grew out of being teased and tormented by our big brother, sister, or the school bully, only to find now at work that there are people (clients, customers, or co-workers) who live to embarrass and irritate us. We'd swear they took a course in "How to Make Janitors Miserable." These ornery sorts exist in every business and can cause real job unhappiness with their continual pettiness and picking away at us. Whether we're saints or sinners, we all have some traits, habits, mannerisms, successes, looks, pay, position—whatever—that bugs certain people and they slip the dagger to us every chance they get.

I've had clients who didn't even know me personally, for example, who consistently and expertly undermined my job for no other reason than they wanted their kids to be doing the cleaning and making the money. In janitorial work other people may purposely leave the place in an incredible mess, hide or sabotage supplies and equipment, set traps, or start rumors and gossip about you. Co-workers may hide out and lounge, shifting all the work onto you, not doing their share while you get the blame.

I don't need to tell you that our job is tough enough without some idiot working overtime to annoy us. Mother always told us to just ignore teasing and the teaser would soon quit, although slugging or some other less subtle form of revenge always seemed more appropriate for such nitwits. But in fact tattling, whimpering, and whining to Mother never got us anywhere and only delighted the tormentor, nor will it help here. Only when we fight tormentors or try to retaliate do they feel fully successful.

The number-one solution is to go on the offense in a different way, **kill them with kindness and good service**. It'll make them look dumb and obnoxious. Create an atmosphere of giving so generously that their own guilt will overcome them and you'll win a friend, not just stop the aggression. Find out what's really bugging them while you're at it, if you can. Maybe it's just your cologne or shaving lotion. You don't have to do this in a head-to-head confrontation: "Okay jerk, what's your problem?" Just do a little gentle investigating to find out why they're after you. Once you discover what it is, you can often eliminate it.

People who are out to get others generally have low self-esteem; they want and need attention. Transforming someone like that into one of your champions is a real accomplishment.

When you have something to say or ask about your work

You don't have to work somewhere long to find a few things to say. Most of us come up with more advice and opinion

than we get—and that's a lot!

We see things that irritate or alarm us, and we all have ideas that would improve the place. We may want to answer criticisms that have been made about us, or need information, supplies, or equipment we don't have. Or we see something being overdone or underdone.

How to communicate things like this, and to whom, is not always a simple matter. Here are a few guidelines I've learned along the way.

1. Above all, first and always, ***before you do anything, make sure you're right and have a worthwhile cause.***

Make sure your facts are up to date and accurate and that what you have in mind is important and needed. Too often when some little thing happens (we find a dead mouse in the coffee pot), we have the impulse to become the "town crier" or at least call Channel 5 Action News. *Think* before you talk or report—some things are best taken care of quietly and privately, or just left to blow over.

When "things aren't running right around here" (the most common complaint/gripe of cleaners), you do want to let people know. Especially if you see something that

could be done better. But be careful. Often things are run much better than you think—you just haven't had a chance to see how it all works yet. You'll just look dumb if you run to the boss with a long list of how he or she should be running things.

2. If you do decide to come forward**, *always approach your own contact person first,*** your immediate supervisor or boss or the person who hired you. Deal directly with them first. Skipping rank or going over people's heads is a deadly game that will get you in the end. The more people you approach or enlist before going to the right person, the more you will worsen and complicate things. About the only value of rank, anyway, is to process communications properly. So go right to your boss, or at most, the next step up, not to fellow workers, attorneys, etc.

3. *Should you say it or write it?*
It's your choice. Lately I've swung around to the written word. When it's right there on the page, it saves time hunting people down and making appointments to see them. And once you write it out, you can make sure it says exactly what you want to say, no more and no less, and no unfortunate unanticipated slips of the tongue. On the other hand, anything written is lasting evidence, so if you accuse or profane or criticize someone, it'll stay around to haunt you forever. Some things should only be spoken.

4. Keep your suggestions positive. Bosses appreciate constructive suggestions, but make sure yours are exactly that—that they're worded or written up in a kind, tactful, and positive way. Don't just make a passing swipe because you're in a bad mood or think you've been treated badly. Provide solid information backed with evidence and your own commitment to help bring your request or proposal to pass. Have a positive attitude, and go to the boss with not just problems but a possible solution or two. You'll be amazed how many things are worked out in minutes, even better than you dared hope!

5. Tattling and tales: Here's a tough one! Should you report, or bring to your boss's attention, things s/he really should know about, though it might mean tattling or ratting on your buddies? Divided loyalty is one of the biggest tests of a professional cleaner. You are bound to be faced with some real conflicts.

There's a torrid romance going on in the janitor closet, or your best friend is using the company computer late at night. Or there's gambling going on in the game room. You don't want to be aware of or

involved in any of this, but you are. What can you do? You can go on your merry way and things will get worse, and eventually someone may be fired, or if the situation is serious enough, the whole company may cave in. Is it better to tell? It's a tough, tough, tough position to be in, and you'll face in it many times.

Be prepared for situations like this in advance by making it clear to fellow workers where your allegiance lies. **Those who are employing and paying you should have your loyalty,** and if you can't give it to them, you shouldn't be working there. Once you make that stand, others won't put you on the spot, because they already know that your first loyalty is to the company, your employer. Then when a problem comes up, inform your contact person of what they need to know, for the good of the company and the preservation of *everyone's* job.

> "If my best buddy is cheating on his time card or stealing stuff, should I rat on him? Shouldn't I be loyal to my friends?" The answer is easy: He or she is the rat, not you or the boss.

6. What if the boss or the company doesn't take your advice? One custodian who fought a garbage problem near the back door for years drew up a plan for the construction of the perfect retainer pad to eliminate the mess. Her supervisor loved it, but when they submitted the idea to headquarters, they said "We don't take advice from custodians." So the garbage kept blowing around and the dogs and raccoons kept rummaging in it. Undaunted, the custodian kept up her campaign for three years. Finally the company did build it; it cost next to nothing and cured all the problems… and headquarters took all the credit for this brilliant idea.

If you do give the boss or company good advice and it's ignored or otherwise abused, don't slash your wrists over it. The same thing that happens to smart custodians happens tens of thousands of times a year to CEO's, professors, mayors, and five-star generals. They don't call it "red tape" for nothing; the red is for the blood let by contributing comrades who were ignored or had the credit robbed from them. It happens to me right in my own company, and it happens to your boss, too. Part of the reason is political, some pettiness, some protection of position. It's not always intentional, often just a careless loss of track in the shuffle of fifty other ideas. Just remember that we never took all our parents', teachers', president's, or boss's advice, either. So live with it and keep advising and giving suggestions. Remember most ace pilots were shot down several times, too. They won their medals going back up again!

When your job starts getting to you

Nothing describes the feelings we sometimes have toward our cleaning job better than this note one of my managers found one day along with the keys.

Ellis was working 14-hour days in the toughest, grimiest, most unappreciative section of the complex we were contracted to clean. He had the worst hours, too. When I saw the note, I didn't blame him— in fact it warmed my heart with compassion.

We've all written similar notes at least mentally when our job begins to match our discouraged mood, and like Ellis, we may even reach the point where it really is

Mr. Stoker,
I have decided
to quit my job! I just
can't take it anymore.
Sorry,
Ellis
Didn't have the heart
to tell you in person!

time to move on. However, every job has its ups and downs, and before you leave, remember that for every Ellis there are about 99 others who at certain times were also on the verge of getting out, quitting, but didn't. And later were darn glad they didn't. I'll bet thousands of janitors a day have left good jobs because they were getting a little battle weary and the last straw was a bad problem that came along on a day when they happened to come to work in a bad mood. The majority of people who quit do it hastily, often over some minor cause, and later regret it. There's not a single person, even million-dollar-a-year ball players, movie stars, ski instructors, doctors, lawyers, and airline pilots, who haven't reached a "fed up" point and wanted to walk away. The dissatisfaction often isn't with the job at all, it's with ourselves or some other personal frustration or circumstance in our lives. So don't be too quick to blame your job and quit it because "It's getting you down."

95

When one of those sour moments comes along (and it will), I'd sure hate to see you yield to some sudden emotion and put yourself out of a job, when you might have found other much less expensive and upsetting alternatives.

This job, your job, **has its costs and risks.**

Policemen get shot, firemen get burned, investment brokers lose fortunes, politicians lose elections, pilots crash, and athletes get torn ligaments and trick knees. I'm sure you know only too well some of the costs that come with the territory when you're a cleaner:

■ It is hard, physically demanding work

■ People take the positive for granted and report the slightest negative

■ We are generally first in line for blame if anything is missing

■ We are often last in line for recognition

■ Our best work lasts only a few hours

■ It seems that the better we clean, the more they mess up to compensate

■ Since no one sees us much, many people don't even know we're alive

■ The pay is often low at the start

■ The working hours are not the same as most business hours

■ It's considered one of the least prestigious jobs around!

These concerns are not going to stop or go away. Right or wrong, they come with the profession. The buildings won't clean themselves, and the occupants aren't suddenly going to stop making messes. All the shortcuts and new equipment in the world aren't going to make our jobs a pushover. Yet if we approach them right, all of these "strains" of our profession can actually be challenging and exciting in the end.

Dealing with the impermanence problem

THEM   5,000 years

US   5 minutes

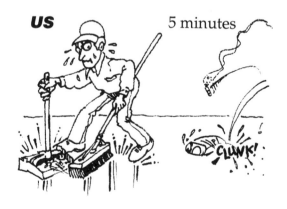

All of us humans have a built in "permanence" drive almost as strong as our hunger and sex drives. We want the things that we own, build, or do (even relationships) to last for a long, long time—if not forever. We get most of our highs in life from the part of our production that lasts and lasts and then lasts some more. Ever since our childhood days of sandcastles, if our work is destroyed right after we do it, we're crushed. We want what we do to last for a while, to be admired and ooohed and ahhed over. Past civilizations worked and built monuments that lasted 10,000 years...

And then there are the janitors, the cleaners. Our best, most beautiful work lasts 24 hours at best, sometimes five hours, sometimes only five minutes. Work we spend hours on is quickly destroyed, often unappreciated. So here it is, the hidden degrader that bugs people about cleaning. The merits of the work aren't lasting, at least that's the way it appears.

People do tear our work down within hours; none of it is visible years and years later like a pyramid or a castle. But here's the key, one of the big secrets of happiness in life: Success is not measured by quantity, how much of something we do or how long it lasts. **Life** is what counts, and we cleaners do something very few people can do. Our work directly affects the quality of life. A doctor with his scalpel or a lawyer with the brilliance of her defense can make someone live longer (increase the quantity of time the person has), but we with a burnisher or brush can affect the quality of that life, how well and happily a person lives. The level of cleanliness we create **changes how people feel and act.** What a compliment. Even if it doesn't last long in physical time, it lasts in the mind, and the heart, and the senses. That makes it eternal and well worth doing.

More cures for the job blahs and blues

You aren't the first and won't be the last to suffer from the job blahs or blues. Here's some good overall advice from my own experience and that of many others who have faced and gone through it.

DON'T

■ Start putting in less time and effort, moving slower, or cutting corners to get even with the boss or the job. That will only end up hurting you and intensifying your guilt and unhappiness.

■ Don't believe all you hear about your friends' "good" and "easy" and "high paying" jobs. Most of those "other job" stories you hear are either untrue or exaggerations. And none of the gory details (hours, dangers, special restrictions, political pressures, etc.) of those other jobs are ever mentioned.

■ Don't hang around with and listen to belly-achers and complainers on the job. The more they moan and groan and whimper and criticize things, the more of that you absorb. Before long you start believ-

97

ing what they say and feeling worse than ever before. Complaining is a cancer that leads to job death.

■ Ever leave your job without notifying the boss or the company well in advance. Some people just get tired of a job or angry at someone and walk off. NEVER, NEVER, NEVER do that, no matter how much you hate the job or the boss. Give a good long generous notice and work hard right up to the last hour. Your record of work and conduct will, in these days of computers, especially, follow you like a shadow... FOREVER.

DO

■ Go to see your boss or supervisor before you go off the rails and talk, don't complain. Just let him or her know you're struggling sincerely for job satisfaction, and it's getting you down. You'll be amazed at the solutions they will have. Hard as it may seem right now, most problems are worked out, not copped out.

■ See if you can switch your schedule around a little, work different hours or a different shift, in a different location or area, or with different people. Learning a challenging new line of cleaning work is often a cure for the blues. You might even transfer to a different city or part of the country—good cleaning people are needed all over. Anything that breaks the routine seems to help us all, especially in cleaning, which like most jobs has plenty of routine.

■ Get a physical. Yes, a health checkup. When is the last time you had one? Two, five, even ten years ago? All kinds of things can slowly happen to our bodies—things like allergies, high blood pressure, arthritis, and heart disease can set in so gradually we're hardly aware of them.

We can even be short of some vitamin or mineral (a doctor can spot this). You'll be amazed what a change of diet or dropping a couple of bad habits can do for your energy level and attitude on the job.

■ Get on good terms with everyone, not just at work but at home. Often it isn't the job that's getting you down, it's something or someone you're at odds with elsewhere and you're carrying it around with you and blaming it on the job. Bad feelings toward someone at home will inject bad feelings into the job every time.

■ Take a realistic look at your alternatives if you left the job today... you'll be surprised how good your job suddenly looks.

Your two basic choices here

If you don't really like the way things are, you have two basic choices:

1. Get out.
2. Get better.

Doing either of these will change your life. Nothing is worse for you or the company than for you to be working at something you don't like. You won't be happy and you won't do your best work. We all know what hard work any job can be if you really dislike it. Some people just never fit in cleaning. They don't like the whole idea of public service, they have no impulse to be neat and clean in their own life, they take no pleasure in it, and so they see nothing in it as a job.

Move up instead of moving on

The world is full of people who are never satisfied with what they have, who jump from one job to another, thinking that somehow "their luck will change" or "their ship will come in." What someone else has always looks better to us, their situation seems softer and richer and more worth having. Yes, the grass always looks greener on the other side of the fence, and when you get there, you often discover it's Astroturf!

> **Instead of changing right now, instead of doing something else, why not get better at what you do? Instead of moving on to a new job, why not move up in the one you have?**

No one, no company, is cleaning as well, as fast, as innovatively as they can or could be. You can be sure your job and your crew could be better and so can your life. You can improve right where you are, and with the Up-provement will come all kinds of bonus byproducts.

Quitting and moving on might not cure you permanently of job dislike (in any job), but I do know the effect that **getting better** in your job will have on you. It does something magic to you, and to the clients and company too. If you are thinking of getting out, quitting, changing from cleaning, before you do, give the "get better" choice a real shot. Do what you have to do to be better or even the best in cleaning, and I promise you that almost every negative of this line of work will go away. You'll love the job, find it more interesting and better paid, and above all, a job where you can and will affect many lives to the good every single day.

So **do more.** Put your head down and into your work like never before and go for it. Move faster, take on some additional responsibilities, be more willing. Doing more is a miracle cure for crotchety cleaners, wait and see.

If you get fired or laid off

It happens… sometimes justly and often unjustly, **we lose our job or position.** Our first impulse is usually to look for someone to blame, beat up, murder, or bad mouth. None of these are good ideas, even if you got a really bad deal. I've had some real injustices inflicted on me that cost me thousands of dollars as well as lost prestige, enough to make a full grown man just lie down and bawl.

But there's really only one good thing to do.

When it happens, calmly ask—and make sure you find out—exactly why the change in your employment was made. You might not always get the full truth about it, but ask for it as sincerely and pleasantly as you can. Understanding the reasons is the only chance you have to fix, change, avoid, or adjust things, either now or in the future. This is beneficial for both parties, and it's the first important step toward growth or getting something else (and you will need something else, for there will surely be a tomorrow, even if it doesn't seem like it right now). In truth most of us who are terminated deserve it, if we would be honest with ourselves, so discovering and correcting the reason should be our first serious pursuit once we get the notice or the news.

WHATEVER YOU DO, DON'T RANT AND RAVE AND STOMP OFF MAD,

AND DON'T BAD-MOUTH THE COMPANY. I'm not interested in hiring anyone who comes to me for a job criticizing the company he or she just left, and most of my fellow business owners feel the same. "Mad" will do you absolutely no good and has a very good chance of blocking future employment. I know it will be tough to hold your tongue, **but do it.** You wouldn't believe how many terminations have been reversed when the fired person turned on some kindness and understanding.

In my cleaning company, for example, we've lost hundred-thousand-dollar accounts and had our best janitors treated disrespectfully. We were doing a good job, but the boss's brother-in-law moved in and needed a job and so he got ours. At first we moaned and groaned and rolled around on the floor and held a "boil the boss in hot stripper solution" meeting… all of that was wasted energy. Then we calmly asked for the reasons why, and made them give them to us in detail. Then in our remaining thirty days, even though we were on the way out, we went to work. We doubled our efforts in cleaning the building; we made it even better than best and went out the door thanking them for what they'd done for us. And we asked them please to call even if there were just some future crumbs that needed taking care of. **No one forgets an ending or leaving attitude**, and as we did in the case in question here, you'll end up back in there, later if not sooner, with a better deal.

When you leave, go in a way that's friendly, clean, honest, and helpful. Even if there's never a chance to get your job back, a good reference from a past employer can take you a long way.

CHAPTER 7

WHERE CAN YOU GO? (For Information, Inspiration, and a BRIGHT FUTURE?)

The "Cleaning" job has been thought of as the end of the line for so many years that most people don't expect much from it. But the world, the country, and every business around is looking for people to become outstanding in their jobs, for promotions, transfers, and new assignments. The cleaning business is no different. All you have to do is make yourself outstanding by your own performance. How do you do that? You know by now there aren't "upgrade your cleaning" courses on every street corner. And if you do find a seminar, you know that getting to go to Hawaii for a week to attend it isn't going to be easy. So you'll need to put out some personal effort to perfect yourself. You can't wait around for your boss, the owners, the union, or suppliers to come in and transform you from a slug to a slugger—it's up to you.

It doesn't matter if you're in charge or one of a crew, a new or an old employee; there are no limits to what you can reach if you do your job better and better. You'll not only be rewarded but sought after, and the knowledge you pile into your head, the skills you train into your muscles, the fight and determination you build in your heart, will add up to things called experience and competence.

Security in life comes from what you are and what you become, not from tenure or politics. Now or later hundreds of opportunities in cleaning, most of which you've never thought of, will appear.

How to better yourself

Here are some of the sources you can latch onto to improve your present job and make yourself stand out!

Maintenance Supplies, 445 Broad Hollow Road, Suite 21, Melville NY 11747; 516-845-2700.

Professional Cleaning Journal, PO Box 810195, Dallas TX 75381.

Sanitary Maintenance, PO Box 694, Milwaukee WI 53201-0694; 414-228-7701.

Service Business Magazine, PO Box 1273, Seattle WA 98111; 206-682-9748.

Services, 10201 Lee Highway, Suite 225, Fairfax VA 22030; 800-368-3414 outside Virginia.

Study time

School isn't out when you are 18 or "when you graduate"; learning should be an important and enjoyable pastime all your life. Start spending some off or idle hours or break time investigating, reading, studying, or getting some further cleaning know-how, how-tos, and what-fors firsthand from other professionals.

Subscribe to as many of the professional cleaning magazines and newsletters as possible. Some are complimentary. Here are the ones I get—write to them for subscription information.

American Window Cleaner, 27 Oak Creek Road, El Sobrante CA 94803; 415-222-7080.

Building Operating Management, PO Box 694, Milwaukee WI 53201-0694; 414-228-7701.

Cleaning Management magazine, 13 Century Hill Drive, Latham NY 12110-2197; 518-783-1386.

EHT (Executive Housekeeping Today), 1001 Eastwind Drive, Suite 301, Westerville OH 43081; 614-895-7166.

Installation and Cleaning Specialist, 17835 Ventura Blvd, Suite 312, Encino CA 91316; 818-345-3550.

Collect cleaning information

Start your own home library and files. This doesn't have to be anything fancy— it could just be a cardboard box at first. Get one and start collecting everything worthwhile you come across on cleaning, newspaper and magazine articles, product brochures and information sheets, government publications, job descriptions—you'll be surprised how rapidly your library will grow. It will cost you little or nothing and be a constant resource for writing, speaking, or your new promotion within the world of cleaning. See p. 183 for some excellent reference books for your collection.

Visit supply stores and look around

Often only your boss or purchasing agent is aware of what's new and upcoming, and he or she won't see all the possible applications you will. So amble down and examine or try out some new equipment, chemicals, tools, pick up brochures, watch demos, etc.

Take advantage of every opportunity to visit other operations or buildings, too. Cleaning businesses are everywhere, and many of them specialize in different types

rules of all the rest. Likewise, we have to know the full scope of our jobs. We may never do bathrooms or carpet, but to be a true pro cleaner, we need to know how. So when you run across an article or a chance to be trained or learn more about some other cleaning area, grab it. You may be promoted to manager or supervisor, or even own your own business someday or want to do consulting, and you'll want and need to know... it all.

of work. Find one up your alley and check with their office when you plan your next vacation. There may be an installation or a building of interest at your destination or on your route. Be ready always to visit and work with other operations. Your fellow cleaners and you can exchange some dynamite information. Ask questions, learn more skills, and make yourself more valuable.

Attend every cleaning and maintenance seminar around

Most are free, and even if you do get a sales pitch, watch and listen and you will learn. And your expanded knowledge will give you an edge.

We cleaners may specialize (see p. 105), but like the doctors, we can't compartmentalize. A foot or an eye doctor may spend most of their time on one area of the body but they have to learn and know the

Give yourself full professional status

There are several associations that make it possible for people with initiative to use some of their spare time to attain degrees and certificates in the cleaning profession. These can be great aids to your career. So write for and check them out when you see them advertised. Many are correspondence courses, and with their help you can have full professional status and some letters behind your name just like those MBA's and Ph.D.'s!

Promotion possibilities

Contrary to the claim that cleaning is a dead-end job, there are hundreds of areas within the cleaning profession that you can advance or work into. In fact, you can even invent your own to suit your abilities and enthusiasms.

> The BIG question we all ask about our jobs (any job) is "Where is this job taking me?" That question is worded wrong. A job will "take you" nowhere. The question to ask is "Where am I taking this job?" A great cleaner, trasher, maid, is a great person, and great people move on and up continually.

No cleaning job is a "dead-end job" unless it's being done in a dead-end way or by a dead-end person. As I mentioned earlier, at one time while I worked for the Bell System (then the biggest company in the world), all five top executives began work as telephone company janitors. I discover again and again, as I speak to large groups of professionals in companies of all kinds, that the majority of those in "high places" worked in cleaning and maintenance-related positions to begin with. Cleaning can and does poise you, not poison you, for progress and upward movement if that's what you want.

In fact, many people have found a niche they love in cleaning, and more money or more exalted positions don't tempt them much. I find this in schools, often, for instance. Many kindly cleaning people there have floods of love and admiration from hundreds of children and have in turn through their work influenced the lives of the students more than teachers, governors, or even parents have. How could you ask for a higher station in life than changing the quality of people's lives? If your job does that and you are happy, you are more successful than any big banker or broker will ever be.

Promotion Preparation

Never underestimate the value of a cleaning job as "the perfect background"

for other jobs, either in or out of maintenance. Lynn Thompson and his wife cleaned a phone building faithfully for five years while they went to college. They loved the job, the people loved them, and they developed habits of punctuality and dependability while broadening their educational base and learning the skills of public relations. Today Lynn is a nationally recognized physics professor and credits cleaning as his real education. The famous Britt Hargraves, speech therapist and lecturer, worked in cleaning for eight years—as a member of a crew, as a boss, as a sales representative, and in the main accounting office of a cleaning company. And even now the best of his great humor and dynamic presentation comes from stories of his experiences as a cleaner. There are millions, in all fields, who got their foundation as a cleaning professional.

The basic procedures for promoting yourself

If you are eager to move up and on to bigger and better things, here are the basic procedures for promoting yourself:

1. Above all, bear in mind that **The key to bettering yourself is getting better. Performance** is what

gives you bargaining power. To better yourself, do the job you're on now better!

If you are ambitious, above all, don't belittle, begrudge, or be lazy on the job you're doing now. Moaning, complaining, and foot-dragging around is the best way to NOT get promoted.

2. Alert your boss or supervisor

that you want change, upgrading, new opportunities—don't assume they know. They might think you are happy as a lark, and even though they want to advance you, not do it. A simple, "Boss, I'm always interested in more work, more responsibility, and more pay" will do the trick.

3. Have a written plan or goal for

what, where, when, and how you want to go. Telling a boss "just better" isn't enough—you need to get specific, starting with yourself. Dig into your personality and needs and try to get to the bottom of **what** it is you want to be promoted to. Type of job or position? Place? Salary? Shift?

4. Learn before you leap. More

often than not, a position will pop up to be filled and no one on the crew of forty cleaners is ready or qualified. So they all sit around dreaming about it, but no one takes the initiative to study, practice, and prepare for it. Investigate what and where you want to go and then make a simple plan for how to get there, a list of the things you have to do to qualify. You can't expect to get promoted just because you are a nice guy or gal, or have tenure—you need to fit the niche you want to fill.

I can't stress enough that the cleaning work you are doing right now is training and grooming and conditioning you for a better future. Working your way up from the bottom isn't just toilet talk. You can't be a master in any field of expertise until you have a feel for the spirit of the work. Character and leadership can come from cleaning the commode in a high rise or a church as easily as from a classroom at Yale or Harvard.

Your Market Choices

Here are some of the jobs, positions, and situations possible within the world of cleaning. Some you might want to set your sights on for a part-time or full-time profession. The pay in all of these still hinges on how well you perform.

You can SPECIALIZE as a cleaner

Specializing: You know what this is; doctors do it all the time. One doctor treats feet or eyes only, another does nothing but deliver babies, another is a specialist in internal medicine. Becoming an expert, superb in one single area, offers many advantages (including the ability to charge a higher fee), and the same is true in cleaning. You'll hear someone say, "I'm a floor man," and that means he's a whiz at stripping and finishing hard-surface floors. He knows the techniques, the machines, and the finishes, right down to how the metal interlock molecules interlock.

You have a big choice when it comes to specializing, because all kinds of places and things need to be cleaned.

OFFICE BUILDINGS

HOSPITALS

GOVERNMENT FACILITIES

FACTORIES AND PLANTS

MOTELS/HOTELS

SCHOOLS OF ALL KINDS

SUPERMARKETS

RETAIL STORES

MALLS

MEDICAL OFFICES

BANKS

PRIVATE HOMES

UTILITY BUILDINGS

MILITARY BASES

AIRPORTS

RESORTS

PARKS

STADIUMS

DEODORIZING

FLOOD RESTORATION

OTHER DISASTER CLEANUP

CARPETS

FLOORS

WALLS

WINDOWS

FIXTURES

FURNITURE

GROUNDS

AUTOMOBILES

MOBILE HOMES

BOATS

and

100's MORE

Full- or part-time jobs in business, industry, and government

There are all kinds of cleaning-related positions you can think about or train yourself for to include in your future in the cleaning industry. Being aware of as many of them as possible will help you zero in on the ones that interest you most. Here are some of the major ones:

CUSTODIAN

In this job you are usually part of a maintenance staff and have a daily cleaning assignment that allows you to experience the satisfaction of a regular job of making things clean and attractive.

MAID

Lots of opportunity and versatility here, working either in homes or commercial buildings. You can work as a maid for yourself, a private client, or a company. Flexible hours and duty assignments. A great chance to design your shift around family schedules and responsibilities, and an excellent part-time or second job. Maid duties are often less strenuous than other types of cleaning jobs.

FOREMAN/ SUPERVISOR

Oversees, organizes, and outlines the crews that clean buildings and care for grounds. A great job for an above-average cleaner who can direct and motivate people and loves leadership. Lots of action and rewards.

MANAGER

Is usually a top-level, multi-building management position. A manager oversees the maintenance operations of a very large facility or a number of smaller facilities. He or she is heavily involved in customer relations and employee hiring, training, and supervision, and is responsible for quality control and meeting of financial objectives.

Single or Site
BUILDING MANAGER

Notice all the big buildings around? Well, just as a train needs an engineer, they all need a manager to direct cleaning, air conditioning and heating, decorating, food service, landscaping, etc. You'd have your own office and a job where you'd learn to be a superb PR and management person.

MANAGEMENT WITHIN A CLEANING SERVICE COMPANY

Contracting services have all but taken over the cleaning of commercial accounts. Cleaning and managing for a cleaning contractor has many opportunities to consider.

BRANCH MANAGER

Totally in charge of the cleaning operations in a city or several areas within a large metropolitan area. Responsible for sales and growth besides all other responsibilities.

DISTRICT MANAGER

In charge of two or more branches of a cleaning company. Participates in major planning and decision-making and has a great deal of independence.

DIVISION MANAGER

Directs an entire division of a company, such as health care, regular janitorial services, security, etc.

ACCOUNTS SUPERVISOR

This is kind of an inspection/public relation slot that many cleaning companies have. You work on quality control and customer service with the building clients.

EXECUTIVE HOUSEKEEPER

Manages the entire housekeeping department of a facility such as a hospital, hotel, etc. An excellent position—flexible, challenging, and interesting, with great pay and advancement possibilities for high performers. A very active and educational job that provides lots of personal contact and life-building experiences.

PROPERTY MANAGER

Many investors buy property, and to make it productive, they need someone to look after it and keep it repaired and retrofitted for clients. A property manager manages both the interior and exterior of the property and administers contracts and leases. Maintenance is the biggest responsibility. In recent years the majority of property managers are women; twenty years ago they were all men! Malls, offices, condos, and apartments are the properties most commonly involved.

MANAGER/DIRECTOR OF PUBLIC BUILDINGS OR PARKS

Ever wonder who runs Yellowstone Park or Mt. Vernon's buildings and grounds? A person like you who has learned to clean well, handle people, and make good decisions. Think of all the beautiful parks in the U.S. and Canada just waiting. You need a few years' experience first, but at 30 you could take over.

TRAINER/TEACHER

Thousands of companies are looking for people well trained in cleaning. Where do they come from? Someone has to teach them. You can set up your own private company or school and offer to run in-house training programs for anyone who needs them. Once you are good and get results, you'll make lots of friends as well as money.

SALESPERSON

Someone has to sell all those cleaning services, all those cleaning and mainte-

nance products and supplies. Why not you? If you have a working knowledge of cleaning and know (or can teach yourself) how to sell, you'll be very valuable to both janitorial and cleaning supply companies. Salespeople get to travel, meet people, make bids and presentations, do demonstrations and training, design and carry out marketing campaigns, and more. There are both commission and salaried positions. Fun as well as potentially very profitable.

YOUR OWN CLEANING BUSINESS

Thousands of people just like you have started their own cleaning companies and contract all types of work from sweeping floors to plant care. You have total freedom to do things your own way and can earn as much as you are willing to put out the effort for. Exciting and more character-building than anything going. No age or geographical limitation. You can start small and hire people as you build your business and sell the company later for a profit.

Everyone considers this at some point. Approach it carefully, consider not only capital but your experience, location, etc. The best helper in making your decision about this is to read *Cleaning Up For a Living* (see p. 185).

Be honest with your current employer

about your desires and intentions to someday do your own thing. When and if you do ever launch into your own cleaning business while you are still working or cleaning for someone else, be especially sure they know about it. Keep it up front and honest so that there is no conflict of interest. Doing it secretly on the side sets off a fuse of suspicion that you are going to quit any day now, or could be using your boss's clients or equipment, etc. Most employers will help you succeed if you are straight forward with them.

Meanwhile be a good and loyal employee in your present job, and do everything you can to learn and expand yourself professionally.

CONSULTANT

After succeeding at any of these careers, you can consult for others—help them solve their cleaning problems and increase their efficiency. (One of the things I consult on is maintenance-reducing design.) Any careers in cleaning can lead to this if you're interested, and you can earn up to $100 an hour.

AND MORE!

You can also:

- Become a **cleaning safety specialist**
- **Write and speak** about cleaning
- Become an **inventor** of cleaning products or processes
- Become an **expert witness** in cleaning
- And yes, the world needs some **lawyers** with a good background in the cleaning business!

PART TWO

HOW TO DO IT:
A PRO CLEANER'S DIGEST
of
Basic
Cleaning Techniques
You Must Know
To Be A
PRO!

HOW TO DO IT:

ORGANIZING yourself and your crew

To clean efficiently we need to be organized, so we can accomplish things faster and better, in smooth order instead of a rushing confusion. "The job" isn't automatically going to organize you. You need to organize yourself before the job starts.

STANDARDS—Your map for managing the MESS

Call them orders, schedules, commandments, specs, outlines, or whatever... there are basically three ways we get our job direction.

Verbal instructions...

Being told and shown what to do, when, where, and why is difficult because we can't always remember the whole process. And even if we do, once some time passes (or we have to reassign the job to someone else), it's a real invitation to error. For small, short-range duties or assignments oral direction is okay. Anything bigger, ask for written directives. If verbal direction is your boss's way, write it down and have him/her repeat it if necessary until you get it all.

Specifications (a guide)...

Specifications simply means the "specifics" of the job—the duties, location,

procedure, and the time of service—are outlined exactly, right down to the frequency for example: "clean the corners once per week." Theoretically, this meets every need, however, no matter how precise the specs are or how carefully they cover all the times and places, in cleaning, things like the condition of a surface, age of a building, the density of traffic that day, weather, emergencies, etc., can't always be foreseen. Specifications can't always keep a place clean. If you find something isn't getting done or isn't being covered, clean it, take care of it, and then talk to the boss or supervisor. Take most specs as general orders and clean accordingly. Specs alone just cannot guaranty a quality level of clean, you've got to use your head as well.

Standards...

With standards you clean not to meet a time or frequency goal, but to achieve a certain level of quality, such as "Keep the corners clean." I love cleaning by standards—it makes more sense and means less wasted motion. Learn to set your own, even if the company you work for doesn't use them. Gradually companies are learning that even the best specs on a building can't cover every aspect of cleaning adequately, so they're using standards. Cleaning to meet a standard is extremely efficient and quality oriented, you clean what is needed, when and where. To help you, your boss, or your customer better understand what standards are and how they are used, I've borrowed a couple standard schedules my company uses from one of my bid packets. These will help:

Item	Standard	Item	Standard
	This building to be maintained at a quality INDEX of 85% or better as per monthly inspection quality rating.	*Fixtures*	Fixtures will be clean, bright, and sanitized, free of odor, dirt, marks, and foreign matter.
Floors	Floors and baseboards will be free of all dirt and debris, removable stains, film, traffic marks, and wax buildup. Floor will have a non-slip finish and a high sheen appearance.	*Waste*	Containers and waste areas will be free of debris, dirt, ashes, and odor.
Carpets	Carpet will be free of any dirt, dust, lint, stain, or foreign matter.	*Dust Accumulation*	No accumulation of dust or fine debris on any exposed surfaces.
Mats	Mats will be free of any observable dirt, dust, lint, or other foreign matter.	*Blinds/Drapes*	Surfaces will be free from dust, dirty marks, and stains.
Walls/Doors/ Partitions	Surfaces, accessories, decorations, and hardware will have a uniformly clean appearance free of dirt, stains, streaks, spots, lint, and cleaning marks.	*Fountains*	Surface will have no streaks, film, or spots. Metal parts will be clean and bright.
Glass	Surface will be kept clean and free of marks and smudges.	*Exterior*	All areas will be kept free of debris and foreign matter. Shrubbery and grass will be kept green, trimmed, and neat. Walks and step entrances will be kept clear of snow and ice.
Lights	All fixtures including bulbs and tubes will be free of insects, dirt, dust, film, and streaks; parts removed must be replaced immediately.	*Supplies*	All supplies, materials, and equipment will be used safely, approved by clients, and properly stored.
Furniture	Surfaces will have a uniformly clean appearance, free of deposits, streaks, film, and removable stains.		

Your Work Schedule

The detailed work schedule outlines all the work that must be done and how often (frequency), to provide the service your company or employer has promised to provide to the owner or tenant of the building you work in. Your work schedule is your best friend when it comes to keeping track of the cleaning tasks that need to be done, and exactly when to do each one.

The frequency work schedule is usually prepared by your supervisor. It outlines exactly what work will be accomplished in each month. It helps assure that the less frequently performed items on the detailed work schedule are scheduled into your regular routine.

Detailed Contract Work Schedule

Days of Service _____
Time Service is performed _____
Building Representative _____

For _____

Work to be Performed

GENERAL CLEANING	TIMES PER WEEK	TIMES PER MONTH	TIMES PER YEAR
Empty and Damp-wipe AshTrays & Urns			
Empty Wastebaskets			
Dust Tops of Desks, Furniture, Counters			
Dust Telephones			
Dust Tops of Cabinets, Picture Frames			
Dust Partitions and Ledges			
Spot-clean or Damp-wipe Desk Tops			
Spot-clean Doors, Light Switches			
Spot-clean Walls, Partitions			
Clean Drinking Fountains			
Clean Sinks			
Damp-wipe Furniture In Eating Areas			
Dry clean Chalkboards (if erased)			
PERIODIC GENERAL CLEANING			
High Dusting			
Dust Venetian Blinds			
Polish or clean Kick Plates and Handrails			
Replace Burned-Out Bulbs and Lamps			
Dust or clean Vents and Grills			
Vacuum Window Draperies			
FLOOR MAINTENANCE			
Vacuum Carpeting - General Offices			
Vacuum Carpeting - Executive Offices			
Vacuum Carpeting - Lobbies and Hallways			
Vacuum Mats and Runners			
Dust-mop or sweep Hard Surface Floors			
Dust-mop or sweep Stairs & Landings			
Damp-mop or spot-mop Floors			
Spot-clean Carpet			
Buff or spray-buff Resilient Floors - Offices			
Buff or spray-buff Resilient Floors - Hallways			
Buff or spray-buff Resilient Floors - Entrance			
Surface Scrub Carpet			
Scrub and Wax Resilient Floors			
Strip, Seal, and Wax Resilient Floors			
Shampoo and/or Extract Carpeting			

Varsity Detailed Contract Work Schedule (Continued)

Work to be Performed	TIMES PER WEEK	TIMES PER MONTH	TIMES PER YEAR
REST ROOM CLEANING			
Empty Trash and Waste Containers			
Re-fill Dispensers (Paper, Soap, Etc.)			
Clean Mirrors and Bright Work			
Clean and Sanitize Sink and Fixtures			
Clean and Sanitize Toilets and Urinals			
Dust Partitions and Furnishings			
Spot Clean Partitions and Walls			
Sweep and damp-mop Floors			
MECHANICAL EQUIPMENT AND POWER ROOMS			
Sweep Floors			
Change Filters			
Dust Low Flat Surfaces (Wall Fixtures, Etc.)			
Dust upper Cable Racks			
Dust Tops of Equipment			
Wax Floors			
EXTERIOR MAINTENANCE			
Sweep Walks			
Sweep Entranceway			
Police Grounds for Trash and Debris			
Cut and Trim Lawns			
Remove Weeds			
Water Lawns			
Sweep Parking Lot			
Remove Snow from Walks			
GARAGE AREA			
Remove Grease Spots			
Sweep Floor Area			
Hose Down Floor Area			
Low Dust Wall Fixtures			
WINDOW CLEANING			
Exterior Windows			
Interior Windows			
Lobby Glass			
CLOSING INSTRUCTIONS			
Arrange Furniture			
Clean Janitor Closet			
Report any Damage or unusual Circumstances			
Secure Exterior Doors and Windows			
Turn off Lights			
Turn on Night Lights			

EQUIPMENT AND SUPPLIES	FURNISHED BY CONTRACTOR	FURNISHED BY OWNER
Buffers - Vacuums		
Cleaning Equipment (Carts, Buckets, Pails)		
Restroom Soap, Paper, Napkins		
Cleaning Chemicals and Compounds		
Light Bulbs and Fluorescent Lamps		
Dust Mops		
Cleaning Rags - Cloths		
Plastic Bags		

SCHEDULING!
There is no one "always right" miracle way to run a cleaning crew

Don't get **overformed!** Forms are simple tools to help chart and organize cleaning operations and keep them "visible." They are meant to help keep track and assign, not confuse! Too many cleaning people go form or computer crazy, thinking that will improve cleaning and scheduling. It doesn't.

Just have a few forms:

1. One pinpointing the areas that are to be cleaned, how, and when.

2. Another recording the hours and logging problems or needs.

3. One more form for ratings and inspections.

Be cautious on form usage beyond this.

Remember to keep it simple, and if your facility has unique needs, design and use your own unique form.

Once you find out what you have to clean, how long you have, what and who you have to clean with, you can make some intelligent plans and start to organize your efforts: work schedules, work loads, storage of tools and supplies, etc. Some people "gang" clean; others single clean. Some do it while customers are there, and some do it during the wee hours of the night. You need to think through the job and all of its needs and then sit down and organize. Always sketch and draw out your lists and plans on paper. Clean the building or area in your mind or on paper before you attempt to make any schedules. Your goals and objectives, the people and equipment you have to work with, and the problems and challenges of every place you have to clean will all have a part in determining frequencies.

If two or three can clean something better and faster as a team than one person alone, bear this in mind when you set up your schedule. For example, two people working together stripping a floor is four times faster than one. Figure out

your own organizational shortcuts like this and use them. (See the chart on the following pages.)

Publicizing your schedule is the best way to get help or fit in new or extra (emergency) work needed. It's also a quick and effective way to transfer your duties in case you are sick, absent, or get moved or promoted.

Some basics that will help

We can't "manage" time, all we can do is learn to use it wisely. Here are some basic preparations that will really help here.

Be early!

Be early in everything you do—going to work, to a call, to a repair, to a meeting. Being five minutes early will generally cut 15 minutes off the time needed to do any assignment (and that will impress bosses and clients!).

Carry with you

Carry with you the tools you will need, not in aprons necessarily, but on a cart or in a caddy. Make sure you select and tailor tools to fit not only the job you have to do, but your own size, weight, and the area you have to work in. Label them clearly for safety and to meet all OSHA and MSDS requirements. Have all your guns loaded, too, that means full containers

and spray bottles, extra vacuum belt, enough cloths. Have everything with you or right in the vicinity of the job so you can spend all your time working, not running back and forth looking for and fetching.

Carry on you (your personal tools)

The small tools you need, have fastened right on you, such as:

    putty knife
    safety glasses
    rubber gloves
    pocket knife
    special keys/codes/cards
    water faucet keys

I also carry a small note pad and pencil for records, ideas, and repair lists to write things down when I see them.

Repair or report it NOW

The worst enemy of efficiency is waiting until later (procrastination). If there is a need or problem it won't go away, it will only get worse, plus take up valuable brain space meanwhile. So whenever possible, fix it when you find it. Leaving a spot or spill for later usually means a worse time to deal with it than right now, and real trouble from the boss and clients.

THE PROS AND CONS OF DIFFERENT ORGANIZATIONAL APPROACHES

SYSTEM/TYPE OF OPERATION	DESCRIPTION
SINGLE PERSON	One individual is responsible for keeping an entire building or unit maintained.
ZONE CLEANING	Each member of a team is assigned to a specific area.
GANG CLEANING	Whole team works in an area at the same time, and each person has a particular task to complete. Team moves from room to room and floor to floor together.
ROUTE CLEANING	Person or team cleans several different buildings.
NIGHT CLEANING	Cleaning duties performed in building after working hours, generally after 5 p.m. and before 6 a.m.
DAY CLEANING	Cleaning done during regular working hours in the building or facility.
DAY PORTER	Auxiliary person available for policing and spotting high-use or high visibility areas, and spontaneous assignments like lights, glass, trash, spills, etc.
STATIONARY FLOOR CREW	Crew that specializes in floors and stays in one building.
ROVING FLOOR CREW	Floor specialists assigned to a number of accounts on a periodic basis.

WORKS BEST	ADVANTAGES	DISADVANTAGES
Small, private, or non-public areas and establishments.	One-on-one communication, clearly pinpointed responsibility.	One person has to have all skills. Absenteeism is fatal. The finished job will only be as good as the individual involved.
Small or specialized areas.	Quality better because each cleaner is responsible for a particular area.	Each cleaner has to be good at everything. Production time slower. Vulnerable to absenteeism.
In larger buildings	Production time fastest, less supervisors needed, group discipline means less dinging and stealing. Saves energy, makes efficient use of equipment, flexible, training easier.	Cleaners need closer control and duties must be carefully synchronized. Quality control more difficult. Hard to pinpoint responsibility when certain areas suffer.
Small accounts or spread out buildings.	Effective use of equipment. Energy advantage. Flexible hours.	Travel cost and risk, vehicle expense, employee time lost to traveling.
Offices and heavy manufacturing.	Unrestricted access. No people delays. Flexible hours.	Security problems, darkness, safety hazards, tired employees.
Seldom used or sparsley populated areas.	Larger labor pool. Security and safety. Energy savings. High production time. Less wasted time and horseplay. Better public relations.	No access to certain areas. Noise and annoyance to tenants.
On spoiled tenants, and in high-use public facilities.	Instant response.	Extremely non-productive, hard to keep cleaners busy or use them effectively.
Large building or complex.	The cleaners know the building and the personnel, no travel cost and risk, easier quality control and security.	Work has to be well scheduled to assure frequency compliance. Takes more equipment for each buiding.
Small or isolated accounts.	Efficiency of scheduling and equipment use.	Travel and vehicle cost and risk, equipment damage, security.

Make your path public

Once you figure out a good order and system for your cleaning—the hours, areas, frequencies, possible close-downs (like restrooms)—write the schedule out and post it and let others know. Then everyone will know exactly what, when, and where. This will also keep you findable. Clients and bosses love that.

Remember!
In/ter/rupt/ions
injure production

Always (every minute!) concentrate on completing a job once you start it. Getting something almost done and then jumping onto something else, or letting yourself be distracted to stop and pick up something or chat with someone, etc., will break your work flow. Anticipate and limit or prepare for interruptions and avoid them. Uncontrolled interruptions can cut your day **30 percent** or more. They burn up the boss too.

Everybody loves you if you do good work and they'll constantly stop to chat or give you extra little jobs. Remember, if you have a building with 480 people in it and each of them only takes a minute of your time, the **whole day** will be used up just visiting!

So once you're on a job stay on it with all your energy. Finish, then switch. Ten-second stops have a way of working into ten-minute delays.

HOW TO DO IT:
WORK PATTERN

If we maintain a clear-cut direction of work we can remember where we are, not forget any desk or trash receptacle, plus keep track of our tools and equipment!

For efficiency and smooth work flow, we clean:

1. Back to front

2. Top to bottom

3. And in a clockwise pattern.

This diagram of an entire floor shows how this pattern is based on the way the clock hands move.

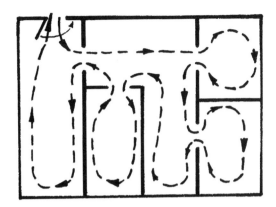

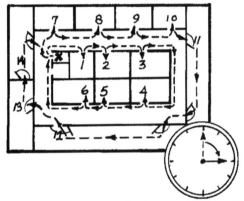

You always clean clockwise, starting at the supply closet and going around the inside offices or rooms one at a time. Once you've worked your way back to the supply closet, go around the outside offices, cleaning them one at a time too—always in a clockwise direction.

A suite, an office which contains several rooms, is cleaned in the same pattern. Clockwise, a room at a time. And an office which consists of just one room also follows the same pattern.

The basic idea of the clockwise system is to start at the back and bring the dirt to the front, so you are never moving from a dirty area into a clean one, and you won't forget where you've been. Example: By vacuuming into a room instead of out of it, you aren't stumbling over cords and carts, they stay in front of you! In restrooms you always work from the cleanest to the dirtiest—trash, sink, partition, toilet, urinal, floor, etc.

Once you get this pattern down, you'll like it, because it helps organize your work.

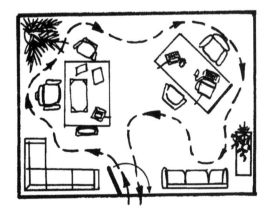

HOW TO DO IT:
BASIC CLEANING PRINCIPLES
Every Professional Must KNOW and Practice

Removal of the soil from the surface is our whole goal, our bottom line. We need to be able to do it fast, effectively, and without damaging the surface while we're at it.

There are some Overall Laws of Cleaning that will help us accomplish this, and they apply to almost every situation. Once you learn them you can adapt them to any job—and do it WELL!

MOISTURE

Or WATER is needed for most cleaning and it seldom hurts a surface if it's only in contact with it for a short time. Left on there too long, however, moisture will work its way into and swell and damage many surfaces. Remember, too, that as water evaporates the active ingredients in your cleaning solution may double and triple in strength. This is especially true of ammoniated products. When in doubt, get the cleaning solution on and off quickly—better safe than sorry.

DRYING

Has to be done right. If something dries too fast it may not do a thorough job of cleaning, or (in the case of something like wax) bond well to the surface; if it dries too slow having the moisture on there so long will warp and rot things. YOU are in control here, so remember: air movement and air circulation (especially of outside air) will dry things faster than still dead air at 100 degrees. Even cool outside air will dry things faster than still inside air. When washing windows, walls, and floors, slow drying is best—for carpet and upholstery the faster the better.

SHINE

You can affect it by what you take OFF as well as what you put on. Shine comes mainly from light reflection. If light will bounce off something it will shine—whether it's clean or dirty. If light is absorbed into a surface (such as cloth), on the other hand, it won't shine. Dirty floors and walls absorb light, so does soap or detergent residue left behind after cleaning. Wear and tear on a floor or other finish can create a porous surface that absorbs light. This is why old things are often dull.

Waxes, polishes, and finishes applied to a surface simply fill in the pores a little and make the surface smoother, so that light will again bounce off, or be reflected from it.

SOILED SOLUTION?

Knowing when to change your water is critical in the cleaning process. How dirty can cleaning solution get and still clean? Detergent and chemical have just so much power to surround and lock onto soils. Once that's used up the solution won't lift dirt or clean like it should. Often you just develop a sense for when it's reached that point. When you can't see a quarter dropped into the bucket, it's time for new solution. Being over conservative beats being over polluted. It only makes sense to clean with clean solution!

HOT OR COLD?

Hot water mixes better with cleaning chemicals and dissolves soil faster, because it speeds up the movement of the molecules. So whenever you can, use hot solution—it means more effective cleaning. Bear in mind however, that once a solution is spread out on a surface (window, wall, counter, or carpet) it becomes room temperature pretty quick, even if it started out boiling hot. Still, warm beats cool when it comes to cleaning. Cleaning with warm solution is generally superior to "chilly dipping" in the old bucket (and it's easier on you, too).

AGGRESSIVENESS

"Scrub," "Scour," "Elbow Grease," and "Cleanser" are militant, violent words in the cleaning vocabulary. Professionals lift, dissolve, and pull off soils, ease and rinse them away. Too often when we come across a stubborn soil we attack it by pushing harder with meaner tools.

"WET" is the key word here. Keep any surface you need to assert yourself on wet. This will soften the soil and lubricate the surface if you have to do any rubbing or scrubbing, so the soil will generally give up before the surface gives out.

AVOIDING OVERKILL

"Overkill" or overdoing it is the worst sin in cleaning—it wastes time and wears out both you and the surface. It also wastes energy and supplies and can harm the environment. If it isn't dirty, leave it alone. If you find yourself on a cleaning schedule that seems to be overkill, talk it out with your boss or supervisor. Do the necessary and see if you can get the overkill reassigned to a lesser frequency. Do the traffic areas frequently, but don't overkill the unused places and spaces.

123

CLEANING 1•2•3•4

(Our Basic Approach to Cleaning Anything)

1 Eliminate

Just as we sweep a floor before we mop it, scrape the dishes before we wash them, clear the counter before we attempt to clean it—apply this principle in all your cleaning. Brush or vacuum, etc. all the crumbs, dust, litter and debris away before you clean. Why end up with all that stuff in your cleaning water, or take a chance of spreading stains? Before you start wetting anything down or going after the attached and embedded soil, remove all the big stuff and anything loose.

2 Saturate

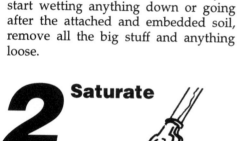

Now put the chemicals to work for you. Spread, wipe, mop, or spray cleaning solution on the surface. Be sure to apply enough to keep the surface wet enough for the chemicals to work, but not so much that it floods and runs. Then let the solution have time to do its job, to soak in and break down and dissolve the dirt and grime. The harder it works, the less **you** have to.

3 Agitate

Cleaning often needs some movement, too, to help loosen the dirt or even just to move it off and away. This is "agitation," as when the agitator in our washing machine churns the soil off our clothes. The everyday word for it is scrubbing, and we do it only when we need to, and with a tool to fit the job (cloth, nylon pad, brush, etc.). When you scrub, bear in mind that EVERY SURFACE—even those that appear flat—has four sides, and we want to be sure to get them all. Scrubbing back and forth or in a circle only gets two sides—so you always want to go NORTH-SOUTH and then EAST-WEST, whenever you scrub. And then repeat.

4 Eradicate

Or REMOVE now all the soil and solution, which we can accomplish by rinsing, wiping with a cloth or sponge, squeegeeing, using a wet/dry vac, whatever it takes to get EVERYTHING (dirt, soil, moisture, soap residue) off the surface.

CHEMICALLY
Speaking

You are, besides an engineer, landscaper, PR person, plumber, painter, guardian, cleaner, or maid… a CHEMIST. The average janitor works with around 700 chemicals and chemical combinations. Chemicals make germs die, rust stop, odor leave, and plain old water clean like crazy. And YOU are in charge of them—their preparation, application, storage, and safety.

So you better…

KNOW

What you're using. You're handed stuff to clean with… chemicals… and for your own good, your health and life, not just your job you need to know what those chemicals are and what they do. The green stuff can be quaternary ammonia or isopropyl alcohol or butyl cellosolve—all used on different things at different times for different reasons. **You've got to know the cleaners you use regularly** as well as

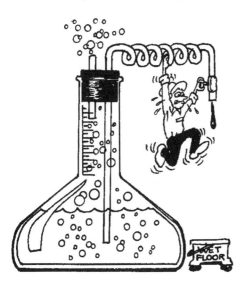

you know your favorite foods: what they contain and what they help and hurt. So STUDY UP and what you don't know, your supervisor, MSDS sheets, spec sheets, labels, brochures, or a salesperson can enlighten you on. You're the one who's going to be using these things—you need to educate yourself.

And

READ THE DIRECTIONS

Amazing, the amount of information right there on the label. The Whats, Hows, Wheres, and What Ifs are all spelled out. Yet not one in 50 of us takes the time (all of 30 seconds) to read and learn what we have here and where to use it, what to do and what not to do. Directions are our road map when we're traveling, and when we tackle a cleaning job, they tell us how to save both building surfaces and our lives. Manufacturers know their chemicals but they can only let us in on what they know if we take the time to read and study. DO IT. Be a 100% direction reader.

USE PROPER DILUTIONS

More isn't always better—the dilution ratio has a lot to do with a cleaning solution's ability to dissolve and suspend the dirt. When you use too much chemical, or too little, you defeat the whole purpose of the chemical, lessen its dissolving ability, do poor work, waste time, and damage surfaces (if not people).

125

60 to 1 for example, means 60 cups of water to a cup of cleaner. The average bucket holds 36 cups of water. That means in this case you'd be adding no more than a half cup of cleaner. A 20 to 1 solution would be a lot stronger.

I know we don't always have the time and means to measure, so we have to "glug-glug," but if we pay close attention the first few times to EXACTLY how much, it'll be a lot easier to hit the mark without measuring. Pre-measured packets of cleaner concentrate are a big help here.

When you're mixing, remember: Too little baking soda in the biscuits means they won't rise; too much ruins them. The same with cleaners—measure your chemicals, don't guess... too much detergent makes your job harder and creates problems.

POST Your MSDS (Material Safety Data Sheets) so everyone knows what a chemical is, what's in it, and what to do if it happens to be misused or spilled, accidently gets in or on us.

The pH Scale

It only takes a minute to learn it, and once you understand the basic principle here you'll have a much better idea of what to use when, where, and why.

The main secret here is that you need to use a cleaner with a pH opposite to that of the soil you want to remove. Many soils are acid, which is why we use alkaline (the opposite on the pH scale) cleaners to remove them. Vinegar is an acid, that's why it won't cut grease (a fellow acid).

When a cleaner is neither strongly acid nor alkaline, but about right in the middle, it's called a neutral cleaner. This is the best all-around cleaner for most jobs and most all-around average soils. And it's pretty safe, both for us to use and for the surfaces we use it on. The higher or lower you go on the scale from neutral, the stronger (and more dangerous) a chemical you're working with.

KNOW THE PH OF YOUR CLEANERS—the label or litmus paper will tell!

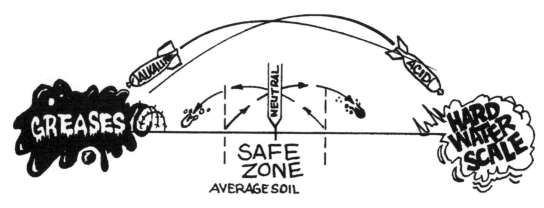

HOW TO DO IT:

The art of
TRASH REMOVAL

Anyone who thinks "dumping the trash" is a half-brained duty doesn't know their profession. It's more than a skill, it's an art and if you don't know the rules you'll never get the job done right. A real pro handles waste and trash quickly and safely. You have to be trained to do that! You can adapt the following guidelines to your specific removal needs.

MAKE IT SAFE

You can get hurt or hurt others while trash handling, so…

1. Don't dump ashes or any hot debris (such as shop waste) into dry trash.

2. Never reach down into a bag or can or push trash down into it with your hand. All kinds of dangerous things such as broken glass, razors, wire, sharp metal, etc., can be there.

3. Don't tromp the dumpster, either. We all do when trash won't fit. It's a bad idea, and many of us have leg scars or bruises from falls to prove it. Stay out of the trash bins. If you have too much trash, wait till there's room for it (store it somewhere else till there is), or order extra dumpsters if they're needed, but remember you aren't a compactor!

4. Don't leave bags of trash sitting "temporarily" anywhere (indoors or out) where people could fall on them or an animal or child could get into them and get cut or punctured.

5. Never block a fire exit with trash or trash equipment.

6. Beware of damaging walls and doors in the course of your waste removal activities! Don't use trash units as a battering ram for doors.

MAKE IT SECRET

What's been tossed
should never tattle!

1. Reading or retrieving trash is unethical/unprofessional. Don't.

2. Hauling or transporting trash around or leaving it anywhere in the open invites it to be distributed all over the county. Seal it up tight to withstand wind, dogs, and rummagers.

3. If in doubt, don't throw it out. We found $150,000 once in a wastebasket (noticed the weight). Boxes of good stuff are often set down in junk areas. **Ask** if it seems valuable!

4. When a 5-10 day trash disposal delay program is the rule (for security reasons) use heavy metal, sealed, and marked containers, not cardboard boxes!

And a real professional knows enough to...

■ Use controllable containers. Too large or too small of a pickup container kills time or kills you. Thirty-gallon Brutes designed for trash are easy to clean and can be rolled on casters, and they sure beat cardboard, canvas, and flimsy plastic containers. Own a good collector.

■ If you can't seem to keep up with an overflowing container, it means you need a larger container or more containers in that area.

■ Keep them clean! Any trash, waste, or garbage left in cans or baskets will generate a terrific sour odor and liquids like coffee, cola, and ink will quickly contaminate your collector. Frequent cleaning inside and out keeps your containers flashy and classy. A kettle brush is a good tool for this. Wet the area, scrub, rinse, and smile!

Keeping the inside of containers clean and slick speeds up dumping, too.

■ Always put the emptied wastebaskets back **exactly** where they belong. If they're moved even a foot from their normal position it will inconvenience or annoy the user. Never set or leave a trash container on a desk or counter.

■ Identify and separate wet and dry

waste, and only use liners on wet—saves time and money. Have rules for wet kitchen trash. Any liquid dumped in dry trash will filter through it instantly, causing staining, sticking, stinking, and time lost cleaning it out of your receptacles. If you do use liners don't leave air trapped under them. If you do, trash disposal will be like trying to eat with a full mouth! Push the liner to the bottom of the can so it fits and leaves the rubbish some room.

■ Always tie off full or complete sacks of garbage or trash.

■ Never leave your container of trash parked in the janitor closet or by the back door. Deal with it now.

■ Always carry trash on stairs.

■ Never drag or scoot bags of trash. They will snag on something and all those half-cups of coffee in there will leak out and stain. Carry or transport them.

■ If the trash is too heavy to lift out (it would ruin your back), tip the container on its side and slide the bag out of the collector!

■ Have an easy-to-reach central disposal area.

■ Arrange a convenient pickup schedule.

■ Require all vending machine suppliers to keep their dispensing machines and area clean (unless it's in your contract).

■ Construction underway in a building will often triple the trash problem. If disposing of it is going to be your responsibility, make provisions for the extra load.

■ Recycling is the right thing to do and it is Here! We custodians get to be the leaders of tomorrow. The programs are new and may be a little confusing right now. Lots of folks in your area may have "show me," "prove it," or "maybe" attitudes about it, and may even refuse to cooperate and make life and litter-sorting miserable for you. Keep working on them and hang on to those recycling programs as they keep coming. They are here to stay, and the new attitudes and consciousness they encourage will make our job easier in the end!

HOW TO DO IT:
Finding delight in DUST REMOVAL

More than 5,000 different kinds of tiny particles (including dandruff, sand, dust mites, parts of bug bodies, lint, hair, and 4,994 more) find their way into the path of we professional cleaners. This all comes together as dust and we find it high, low, under and over almost everything we clean. It hurts people's pride more than it does the surface where it rests, but it has to go!

When I introduced contract cleaning to the Bell System (and their more than 35,000 buildings) I was in turn introduced to a more scientific approach to dust control. Here, to keep everyone happy we had to keep dust out of the sensitive electronic equipment as well as the offices and furnishings. And with the advent of clean rooms, dusting has taken on a whole new meaning.

If left, dust doesn't just lie there harmlessly, but is constantly stirred and circulated. Those minute particles swirl around in even the tiniest air currents indoors (even just the draft created by a person walking by), and as it collects dust mars surfaces (some of those tiny particles are sharp), plugs filters, and magnetizes it-

self to computer monitors. Dust is particularly attracted to warmth. If dust sits on a surface for any length of time it combines with airborne grease into a stubborn sticky film. It's our job to find it and capture it before that happens!

CAPTURE

We used to think that knocking dust off the most visible surfaces with a feather duster was enough, but all that did was redistribute it to hurt buildings and haunt us further. Our job isn't to move dust around, it's to move it out. Many people think a wet mop or a damp dust cloth gets it all. That's somewhat deceptive. Dust-saturated cloths, even wet ones, will leave dust behind (and you'll see it as soon as the surface dries). You still have live dust! Some try to "blow" dust out of closed areas or from sidewalks. Where does it go? If it's not captured, it returns. The vacuum is one of the greatest capturing tools.

PREVENT

1. Matting entrances inside and out can capture up to 80 percent of the potential dust that just walks into a building. See that all entrances are matted and that the mats are cleaned regularly. Make sure they're being used to the max. Mats should be long enough to allow for four steps, see illustration.

2. Change vacuum bags before they're packed full and use the brand of bags and filters recommended by your vacuum's manufacturer to keep dust contained once you've sucked it up.

3. Change filters on all HVAC equipment per the manufacturer's recommendations. That traps dust in transit.

4. Dustmop right after spray buffing to nab powder before it drifts to new resting and hiding places.

5. Open windows and doors invite outdoor dust, keep them closed.

HOW OFTEN?

Determine dusting frequencies by how fast it accumulates. A limited use, air tight building may only need dusting on a weekly or monthly basis. Heavy traffic or an older building may call for daily dusting. As a pro you need to determine the frequency and make sure your supervisor knows it. Then follow the schedule.

Dust Rhythm Rules

■ Start at the top, work to the bottom. Do high dusting first and end with low dusting.

■ Dust before you vacuum, so the vac will pick up the dead flies, etc., you knock to the floor.

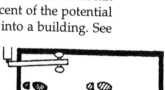

- Lead with your left hand, pick up an object, dust it with the cloth in your right, dust under it, then replace it.

- Work your way clockwise around the room so you don't miss anything.

- Do picture frames and window moldings as you go.

- Don't forget the backs and rungs of chairs.

- Avoid oils and polishes on your cloth, they just help the surface attract more dust!

DUSTING TOOLS

Masslinn dust cloth

This disposable dust cloth was developed by Bell laboratories for maximum dust retention. It's a lightly treated 24" x 24" paper-type product that doesn't leave a sticky surface. It picks up and holds dust particles, and when it's saturated just throw it away. Masslinns are used in hand dusting and on floor sweeping tools. A pro tool indeed, available at janitorial-supply stores. They will leave a slight film on glass.

Electrostatic dust cloth

An untreated cloth developed by DuPont that picks up and holds dust by static cling. When it gets loaded up it can be laundered and reused (up to a hundred times.) The brand name is New Pig, and these dust hogs leave no film. You'll want one of these with you at all times.

Lambswool duster

This cotton-candy-like puff of lambswool reaches into louvers, vents, blinds and irregular surfaces, gets the corners, cracks and crevices. It grabs and holds cobwebs, too. It's so light you can use it on things like lampshades and light fixtures. The long handle enables you to reach things easily, and if you attach it to an extension handle you can even reach ceiling beams and chandeliers. When the duster head is saturated give it a good shake over the dumpster outside. When it's really dirty you can give it a shampoo and rinse, then spin the handle between your hands to get rid of the bulk of the water. Then let the duster air dry.

Feather duster

Just the thing for a shelf of delicate figurines or other small pieces too numerous or delicate to pick up and dust individually. Starting at the top, gently use a feather duster to flick dust to a lower level and eventually the floor where it can be vacuumed up. Feather dusters are useful in retail stores. Genuine ostrich feathers work best because they do capture some of the dust. When the duster head is loaded up, shake it outside or gently vacuum it.

131

NOW FOR AN OFFICIAL CLEANING
SAFARI

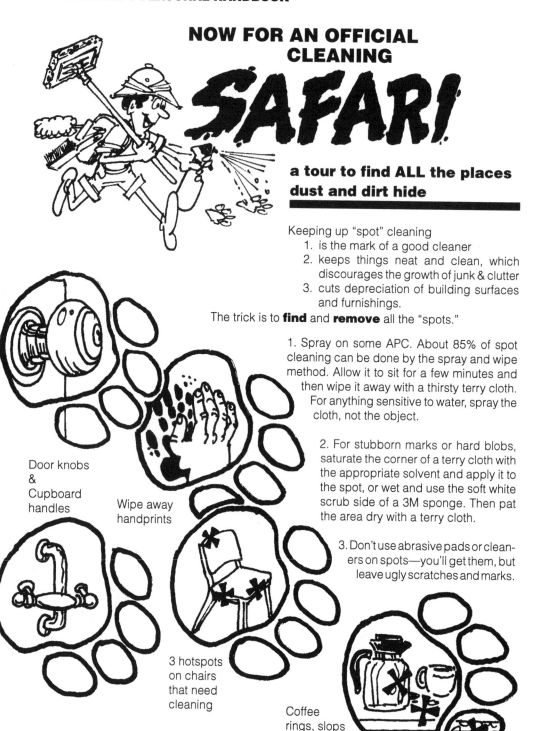

a tour to find ALL the places dust and dirt hide

Keeping up "spot" cleaning
1. is the mark of a good cleaner
2. keeps things neat and clean, which discourages the growth of junk & clutter
3. cuts depreciation of building surfaces and furnishings.

The trick is to **find** and **remove** all the "spots."

1. Spray on some APC. About 85% of spot cleaning can be done by the spray and wipe method. Allow it to sit for a few minutes and then wipe it away with a thirsty terry cloth. For anything sensitive to water, spray the cloth, not the object.

2. For stubborn marks or hard blobs, saturate the corner of a terry cloth with the appropriate solvent and apply it to the spot, or wet and use the soft white scrub side of a 3M sponge. Then pat the area dry with a terry cloth.

3. Don't use abrasive pads or cleaners on spots—you'll get them, but leave ugly scratches and marks.

Door knobs
&
Cupboard
handles

Wipe away
handprints

3 hotspots
on chairs
that need
cleaning

Coffee
rings, slops
and spills

132

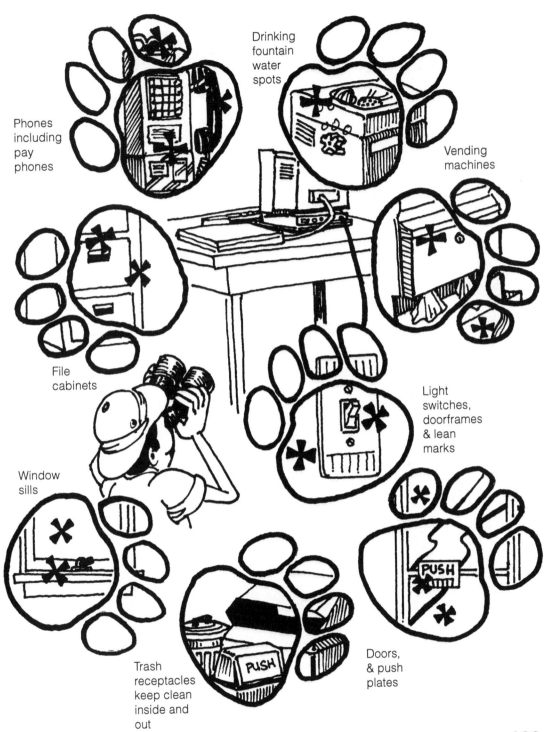

Phones including pay phones

Drinking fountain water spots

Vending machines

File cabinets

Light switches, doorframes & lean marks

Window sills

Trash receptacles keep clean inside and out

Doors, & push plates

PUSH

PUSH

HOW TO DO IT:

FURNITURE AND FIXTURES

To our tenants the building is merely the place or space they work in, but the furnishings and fixtures they tend to get possessive about and adopt as their personal property. Furnishings are used directly by people. This makes them super sensitive about how those furnishings are kept. A shiny floor may go unnoticed, but a shiny desktop or credenza is up close, right there under their nose and at their fingertips. As you clean for people, you'll find it amazing how a little dust on furniture will be noticed more than a lot of dirt in other places.

DAILY

Dusting, spot cleaning, and damp wiping as necessary

Will keep fixtures and furnishings in good shape. Report or fix any damage or breakage.

Furniture's biggest enemy is using too much polish. This just leads to a streaky, gunky buildup. Far better to just damp-wipe the surface and polish it dry—don't over-apply waxes and polishes.

DEEP CLEANING

Vacuuming, washing, polishing, moving and cleaning behind—can be done monthly or twice a month, according to how much use and abuse the area gets.

Specific surfaces

Plastic Laminate ("Formica")

Is the surface most often used in the workplace. That's because it's tough and easy to clean and keep looking good.

To remove the daily buildup of fingerprints and smudges, etc., just wipe with a cloth dampened in a light solution of APC and follow with a dry cloth.

Metal

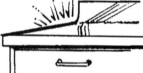

Metal furniture can be dusted, cleaned, and polished all in one step with fast-evaporating alcohol-based glass cleaner.

When tarnished use a gentle polish like Nevr Dull or Brasso. Some surfaces appear to be metal and are not. When metal polishing, I start or experiment in an inconspicuous place so if something is unpolishable I'll know before it's too late. Keep metal polishes of any kind off adjoining surfaces such as wood or cloth. That "black" that comes off when you're polishing is oxidation. Apply the polish or paste as per directions on the container and wipe with a cotton terry towel. Repeat until all the black goes and the metal glows!

Glass

For glass furniture, use a fast-evaporating glass cleaner such as Windex. Spray it on and wipe it off with a dry cloth.

Leather

Dust or wipe quickly with a cloth lightly dampened with APC. Never spray solution directly on leather, or flood it with water. Saddle soap (see manufacturer's directions) is a good way to deal with accumulated dirt on leather.

Wood

Careful! You need to know if the finish on the furniture is strong enough to keep out moisture. There is a danger that water will penetrate the finish and raise the grain, or soften the glue on veneer. If the wood is varnished, clean with a damp cloth and APC, just as you would Formica. If the wood is raw and unfinished, or oil treated only, you need a penetrating type of oil to condition and preserve it. Use the assigned or recommended type at the recommended frequency.

Always use the same brand of polish and it will be self-removing and won't build up or cloud. Spray the cloth and wipe away dirt and oils, turn to a clean side of the cloth and wipe again with the grain.

Fabric

Vacuum frequently to remove the airborne dust and grease that settles and accumulates and causes wear. You can protect arm and headrest areas with covers or Scotchgard. Wipe head/arm rest areas occasionally as needed with a shampoo-dampened cloth, and be sure to rinse with another damp cloth or towel to avoid leaving soap residue.

Spot clean immediately—don't wait (see p. 153). Remember to blot, don't scrub.

Upholstery cleaning is a whole market in itself that has lots of room for profit. If you decide to get into it, study up and chose an extraction machine that leaves little room for error.

Vinyl

The easiest! Wipe with APC. It won't dull and dry out the finish.

CARING—small touches that save you!

A person's home is his or her castle and so is their desk! Leave it as you find it—minus the dirt of course. If a desk is strewn with papers and projects, leave it alone. If it's clear then make it clean. Pick up objects with one hand (the paper clip or pen holder, plant, or picture of the kids) dust under it and give the item a once over with your Masslinn dust cloth in the other. Put everything back exactly where it was. Moving a desk accessory to another spot—even an inch away—will really upset some people. Making this a strict habit here means you'll never have to pay for something you've misplaced. Never set tools, cleaners, wastebaskets, or chairs up on furniture tops or upholstery when you're cleaning underneath. You never know what will leak, scratch, or mar the finish.

Accidents do happen, and if you break

something or move it for any reason be sure and leave a note. You don't want them calling in the FBI just because you've taken something to be repaired. GO SLOW when moving furniture—carelessly bumping it around is what causes most damage. Clean all sides of the piece and the spots where the legs rested, and if they were on carpet brush up the nap. Furnishings have a point of no return where no amount of cleaning will bring them into shape. It's up to you to point this out when and if a client is blaming you for not restoring the appearance of something. Report any damage you come across IMMEDIATELY.

THOSE SMALL TOUCHES THAT CAN SAVE YOU

✓ Clean the desktop if it's clear
In general, clean around things, don't move them. If that's not possible, ask if it's okay to move whatever has to be moved to clean.

We all use the proceed with caution rule here. Be sure to adjust, realign, and straighten things as you go—leave nothing sideways, crooked, or leaning.

X Put everything back exactly where it was on a desk.
Moving things even an inch out of place will really upset most clients. Furnishings and project piles, etc., are mighty personal stuff.

*!# Never lay or sit anything on furniture or fixtures.
This means equipment or cleaners such as spray bottles, sponges, or buckets as well as clothes or coffee cups. Never set chairs or wastebaskets on desks, even to get them out of the way so you clean under the desk.

M When you move it, clean it.
When a furnishing or fixture has to moved for some reason, take advantage of the chance to clean all the sides and the floor underneath. And whenever you move anything, go slow. Moving does more damage to furniture than anything.

? ASK first!
All furniture and fixtures someday reach the point of needing repair, reconditioning, or replacement. When that time comes, suggest it or point it out, but never do it without permission.

! If you remove anything
from a room you're cleaning for any reason (it broke, you sent it off for repair, etc.) be sure to leave a note. You don't want to see someone get excited and call the FBI because you took a lamp or credenza without informing anyone.

Cleaning all those UNIQUE decorations,
trophies, sculptures, pictures, posters, knickknacks, and hundreds of other little you-name-its...

Desks, walls, floors, and offices we know and can clean fast and well, but when these same surfaces are covered with decorations and obviously treasured trinkets, we are often halted to ponder their preservation before we can pursue our duties any further. It would take 900 cleaning volumes to cover every possible piece and its makeup (leather, velvet, cast iron, fossil rock, silk, fur, etc.), so let me share my own personal rules about such things with you:

1. First ask and find out if they, the owner, really expect or want you to clean that whatever on their wall or desk or in the closet or corner. Often these things truly are personal treasures and they would rather do it themselves. Ask!

2. If it is indeed in your ballpark and you don't know how to go about it, ask the owner, supervisor, or manufacturer what the recommended way to clean it is, what you can and cannot use on it, etc. This will help prevent both shaky nerves and liability.

3. Assess how old, delicate, and expensive it is before tackling it. Will it fall apart (and if it does, can you put it back together?). Can you even move or lift it? If in doubt, get help.

4. Study and identify the surface of the object, especially, before you start. Do this by looking, feeling, smelling, thumping, reading, inspecting, etc. Carefully test the cleaner you plan to use with a white cloth in an inconspicuous spot if you have any doubts.

5. Remember that you don't have to clean things in place, right in or around the spot they happen to be. Most decorations are movable to a safer, nonsplashable, easier to reach position or location. When you do, place a cloth or towel under the object to pad it so that being tipped or bumped won't hurt or break it.

6. Whatever you do, go slow and careful.

7. You generally want to clean things like this as dry as possible. This means vacuum and/or dry clean with a dry sponge. If you must do wet cleaning, apply as little solution as possible gently, and then remove it gently by blotting and

137

absorption, rather than rubbing or scrubbing. Always use white cotton cloths so you can stay alert for color fastness, and see whether or not the dirt is coming off.

8. Be extra careful not to leave a residue of soap or detergent behind on the surface of things like this, so they won't get sticky and collect dirt faster.

9. When you're done, leave a note or acknowledgment that you cleaned it, to make sure they know and will appreciate it (and you).

10. Be sure to hang or place any object back *exactly* where you got it.

P.S. If you ever do damage or break anything, be sure to report it immediately. Don't ever try to hide it, or put it back in such a way that the next person who grabs/touches it will think they broke it. Face the music immediately, it's never as bad as your imagination works it up to be. To clean things you have to work on them, and handle them, so you're bound to break or ruin something sometime.

HOW TO DO IT:
WALLS AND CEILINGS

Our disposable society hasn't stopped at paper plates. Many home and building owners handle their walls and ceilings the same way. When they get dirty, spotted, and smudged, they repaint or replace them. But most walls and ceilings can be cleaned quickly and easily, while paint-

ing is at least 80% more expensive and replacement up to 500% more!

Just about any type of wall or ceiling can be cleaned with the right tools and techniques.

WALLS

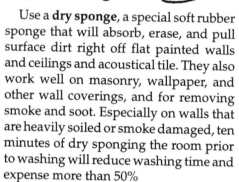

Dry cleaning

Use a **dry sponge**, a special soft rubber sponge that will absorb, erase, and pull surface dirt right off flat painted walls and ceilings and acoustical tile. They also work well on masonry, wallpaper, and other wall coverings, and for removing smoke and soot. Especially on walls that are heavily soiled or smoke damaged, ten minutes of dry sponging the room prior to washing will reduce washing time and expense more than 50%

One swipe of a dry sponge will remove the dirt. It won't remove fingerprints or flyspecks—only the film of dirt. To use a dry sponge just get to the surface and swipe in four-foot lengths, or shorter if your arms are shorter. The sponge will absorb the dirt and begin to get black. A dry sponge has eight good surfaces, if folded and used correctly. When it's black on both sides, throw it away.

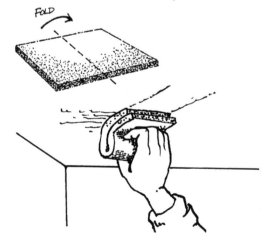

Wet cleaning

Most paint, tile, wall covering, wood, and stainless steel found on walls can be washed. With this two-bucket system you can wash an entire house or building with one bucket of water and a few cents' worth of cleaner, and never change the water once.

The five things you need

1. a bucket of warm water with appropriate cleaner

2. an empty bucket

3. a sponge

4. a terrycloth cleaning cloth (see below)

5. and a dirty wall!

To wash a wall

1. Use a prepared solution, or put a small amount (read label directions) of neutral cleaner into half a bucket of water. For greasy areas, use heavy duty cleaner or degreaser.

2. Dip a damp sponge about half an inch into the solution.

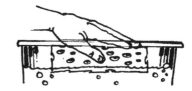

3. Start at the top and apply the solution evenly over about a 4' x 4' area, or an area

How to make a cleaning cloth

Get some heavy cotton terrycloth, preferably white (old towels are fine for this). Cut it into 18" x 18" squares. Hem all the edges of each square and fold it in half. Then sew the long side together firmly and you'll have a "tube" of terry. Fold it once, then again, and it'll just fit your hand. As you use it, it can be folded and refolded and then turned inside out to give you 16 fresh sides to clean with.

These can be washed and dried (make sure they're tumble dried) and reused over and over.

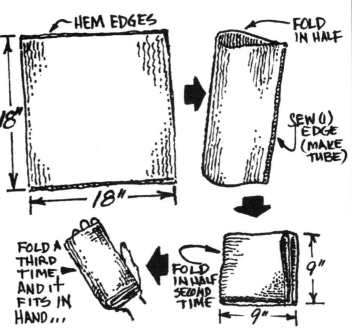

HEM EDGES

18"

18"

FOLD IN HALF

SEW (I) EDGE (MAKE TUBE)

FOLD IN HALF SECOND TIME

9"

9"

FOLD A THIRD TIME AND IT FITS IN HAND...

5. Squeeze (don't wring) the sponge into the empty bucket.

6. Dip into solution again and repeat the whole process.

Don't concentrate on tiny areas and scrub in one place. Cover a large area at once. By the time you get back to where you started, the solution will have softened the dirt.

A little more wall washing wisdom

- Use your lambswool duster to remove dust and cobwebs before you start

- Dry sponge the wall first, before washing, if it's extra dirty

- Consult the manufacturer's recommendations if you are in doubt about how to clean a particular type of wall covering

- Keeping the bucket no more than 1/2 full will reduce the chances of tipping and spillage.

- If the solution runs down the wall, you have too much liquid in the sponge or are pulling too hard on the sponge.

you can reach comfortably, and give it a few seconds to dissolve the soil. Then go back over the wetted-down area with the sponge to remove the soil.

How far you can reach, the amount of air circulation, etc., will determine how big an area you can wet down without it drying on you before you're through.

4. Wipe the sponged area with a folded towel to polish it dry.

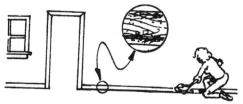

Cleaning painted woodwork

Just wash with solution and dry with terry towels. To pick up all that the lint and hair always on the baseboards, wipe with a used damp cleaning cloth or paper towel before you start washing.

Textured wall coverings

Will always have plenty of dust and dirt down in the millions of tiny indentations of the design, and it will spread out all over if the wall is wet or rubbed. Always vacuum walls like these before wet or dry cleaning.

Paneling

Clean same as painted walls, using a sponge lightly dampened with neutral cleaner or oil soap solution. Buff dry immediately with a cleaning cloth, wiping with the grain.

Vinyl wall covering

Apply the cleaner recommended by the manufacturer, with minimum moisture, especially near the seams. Never use abrasive cleaners and be sure to dry thoroughly immediately after washing.

CEILINGS

Ceilings are a lot harder to wash than walls, so whenever possible, get by with dry sponging. If a few flyspecks remain, dip a cotton swab in white shoe polish or matching paint and mask them. If a ceiling poses a major cleaning challenge because of its texture or stains from water leaks, tobacco, or other sources, seal the stains as necessary with shellac and roll a coat of paint on it.

Use the wet cleaning process as you do on walls only if the ceiling has sufficient paint to hold out the moisture. Otherwise it will penetrate to the sheetrock and make a mess.

When you wash a ceiling do all around the edges first, then the middle. Overlap a couple of inches into the previously cleaned area when you polish the new area dry, to reduce the possibility of streaks. On enamel ceilings sponge-rinsing may be necessary to avoid streaks.

Acoustic tile

Ceilings should be dry sponged yearly—once they begin to look bad it's usually too late to clean. You can paint an acoustic ceiling, but it usually ruins both the looks and the acoustics. There are all sorts of acoustical ceiling cleaning companies and franchises around today. They can give you a bid if you cannot get to the ceiling yourself. Basically, they spray a bleach-type solution on the tile and it whitens it. The place will smell like a swimming pool for a while, but this method works fairly well. Sometimes the price of such cleaning is high enough that it is cheaper to replace the tile. Height and access is a big factor on ceilings. If you can't reach them safely or are afraid of heights—stay away from the ceiling!!

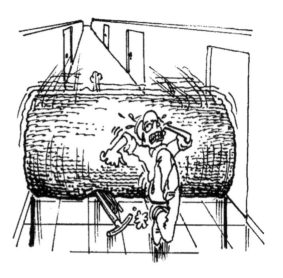

Remember, YOU clean it regularly, so YOU need to know carpet better than anyone. It's your responsibility to watch it, care for it, and notify others of its condition as necessary.

HOW TO DO IT:

A Professional View of CARPET

Thirty years ago, 90 percent of the floors in the buildings we serviced were hard surface floors. Our cleaning concerns were choosing and caring for the right finishes, and spots and stains were taken care of by a simple wipe or mop. Today many buildings are 90 percent soft flooring, or carpet (even in the cafeterias and storage rooms, and on the walls!).

Carpeting is such a safe and quiet surface, but the care of it can easily sneak up on you, if not past you. Spots and stains now consume up to 20 percent of our cleaning time and can still look bad when we're done. We are bombarded with carpet restorative and preventive programs, and we have the choice of ducking and running, or learning carpet care.

Learn all you can

Carpet knowledge is available, in seminars and books, from manufacturers, salespeople, and those seasoned in carpet care. It's entirely to your benefit to dive in and soak up all the carpet wisdom you can. These skills will benefit you personally, as well as your company. Here are some carpet basics, but I encourage you to take it upon yourself to secure and learn the details.

The Preventive Program

Upfront care of carpet means less cleaning and repair!

Mats

Make sure good walkoff mats are down, inside and outside every entrance. See that they are kept clean so they can do their job efficiently. This greatly reduces carpet damage and soiling.

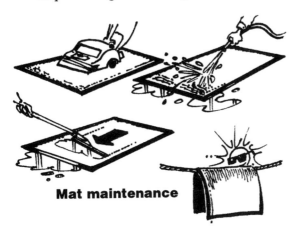

Mat maintenance

Retardants

Use soil retardant wisely. All new carpet installed these days has it, but it will wear off in time. Retardant has to be reapplied to carpet that has received hard use or been shampooed. You can have a pro do it or learn how and do it yourself.

Schedule

More frequently used areas need more frequent service. We have a tendency to clean by room—do it by area. Heavy foot traffic/food areas should have almost double normal area service.

Repair

Report or repair any carpet cuts, threading, bubbles, loosening, or split seams immediately. A timely $5 repair can save a $500 replacement.

Spotting

NOW is the magic word. A spot is on, and a stain is *in*. If you clean up that spill now it'll go fast and there'll be fewer stains left behind. Getting to spotting right away saves time and it saves carpets. Keep your spotting kit handy and know how to use it.

Our goal is to KEEP carpet at a constant high level of appearance. An up and down cycle is unsightly, unsafe, deteriorates the carpet, and wastes time and supplies.

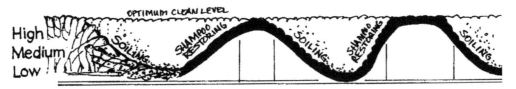

The low care level is the realm of fast deterioration, tough cleaning jobs, and COMPLAINTS!

Cover

Any area where things like painting, repairs, and construction are going on. Cover the carpet with a canvas tarp to stop soiling, staining, and snagging. 4' x 8' sheets of masonite work well, too.

DAILY carpet care

Standard:

Carpet should at all times be free of dirt, dust, lint, stains, and litter, and there should be no snags, loose pile, or exposed seams.

These are general guidelines—you will of course want to adjust for your specific building/situation.

Frequency:

Underkill and overkill are equally bad for both the carpet and for us. There can be no one set schedule for all carpets—the number of occupants and users of a building, and the type of use it gets (whether it's a doctor's office, church, factory/plant, or office) can make a big difference in cleaning needs. As a rule, we vacuum high-traffic areas daily, medium-traffic areas three times a week, and remote carpeted areas, once a week to once every two weeks. Remember, even carpets that aren't walked on still get some building fallout (including dead bugs, HVAC unit debris, etc.), so they need vacuuming.

VACUUMING

The popularity of carpet in commercial buildings has made the vacuum cleaner our most important weapon in the battle against dirt. We have no choice but to become expert with this valuable yet vulnerable tool. Most of us will vacuum millions of square feet of carpet in our lifetime of pro cleaning, so we need to know how to use this vital machine—well!

Which vacuum?

I know that often we're just handed "a vacuum" and have to learn to use what we have. That's okay until we have a chance to change to something that fits the type of job we're doing. Whenever possible, you do want to use the right vacuum for both you (your size, weight, strength, etc.) and the job (area or application). It makes a big difference in the speed and quality of your work and prevents damage to the surroundings, too.

Suction alone won't remove deep soil. A vacuum needs two things to clean carpet efficiently: beater bar action to loosen deep-down dirt, and a current of air ("suction") to carry the debris into the bag. All good uprights have beater bars or brush rolls, and canister vacuums have them in their power heads. A beater dislodges embedded dirt and soil so the suction can pull it up into the vacuum.

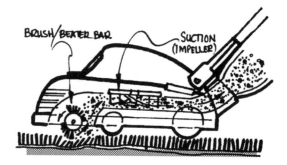

The Basic Choices

HAND

Quick and portable for small jobs. A good vac to keep near the action.

CANNISTER

For above-floor vacuuming and work that requires special attachments.

For shop and warehouse work a tank vacuum is necessary. A wet/dry is best.

UPRIGHT

You want a strong commercial model with at least a 6.5 amp motor and a 50-foot cord.

GIANT

Space vacs are best for big open unobstructed areas.

BACKPACKS

There are times and crowded places with low-pile carpet where these are the answer. Try one if you've been wondering.

CARPET SWEEPERS

Are light and handy just a quick fix for "popcorn" type litter. They don't pull dust and dirt out of the carpet, so don't get in the habit of overusing them. They can't replace a real vacuum!

Remember: **YOU are the pro**—you have to know and tell (persuade) the boss what the best vacuum is for what you're up against. Thus gradually you'll customize and speed up the process.

The Pro Approach to VACUUMING— tested trade techniques you need to use

The biggest pro secret: Vacuum all carpets and mats **regularly!** Don't wait until you can see the dirt. Because it may be possible to camouflage crumbs, dog biscuits, pins, pennies and peelings in a thick luxurious pile doesn't mean you should overdo it. All materials detrimental to carpeting should be kept out of it. Proper timing of vacuuming can extend the life of carpet and reduce the need for shampooing up to 50 percent.

Before you start, get up all those things you know aren't going to be gobbled up by the vacuum—bolts and forks and boots just won't make it, nails or needles either. Pick up things like this before you start and you save time as well as your vacuum cleaner.

Slow down... it's faster in the long run. One leisurely stroke will beat five quick swipes any day. Take your time and let the vacuum work for you. It needs time for the beater bar to loosen the dirt and for the air flow to suck it up.

Vacuum in front of, not behind you. Vacuum into a room, for instance, not out of it, so the cord is behind you and you don't run into things.

Traffic areas should always get your efforts 3 to 1 over any-where else. It's the heavy

wear areas (where dirt is ground in) that depreciate the fastest and need the most attention—daily, if they get daily use.

The edge—don't sweat it. What little dirt and dust there is on the edges of the carpet and under and behind things doesn't hurt anything. Where the vacuum won't reach and the foot never treads, don't worry about it unless it looks bad. It's the grinding in of dirt underfoot that cuts and abrades and damages carpet. Once every two weeks, before vacuuming, sweep along the baseboards to flick any accumulated dust and debris out where the vacuum can reach it. Get those corners and edges with a canister vac and a crevice tool as needed.

Stairways don't have to be a pain to do and the easy way to keep stairs and corners vacuumed is to sweep or wipe them with a damp cloth, then use a tank-type vacuum with a long hose and a small upholstery tool attachment on the end of a "wand" every three months or so. True, there is no beater but in this case, the stronger suction from the small attachment and vigorous hand action does just as well. Using your upright vacuum on the stairs where it can be done safely will prevent dirt from accumulating in the traffic areas.

Vacuums aren't battering rams, but most of us end up using them like that—nicking, scraping, and gouging baseboards, furniture, and doors in the process. IF the rubber bumper guard is in place, a slight bump won't mark or mar anything. Missing or nonfunctional guards are the biggest single cause of ruined facilities and client complaints. Eighty percent of vacuuming problems are caused by a loose nut on the end of the handle. Don't you be one!

Carry your vacuum over tough terrain. They aren't 4 wheel drives—pushing and dragging them across any rough terrain such as sidewalks or hard tile floors, really tears them up.

THE BOTTOM LINE.

The noise.... You get used to it, but others aren't. Be considerate when people are speaking, on the phone or in conversation. Especially if your machine develops a high whine because the fan is wearing out or the bearings are going.

YOUR VACUUM'S Health Checkup Chart

A professional tool like a vacuum has to be tuned and running perfectly to pick up dirt and time. You are the sole responsible party for this—never just use your machine till it quits. Keep this important machine in perfect shape. Here's a checklist that will help.

✚ Don't let your bag "overeat" Anything over 20% full will sap its cleaning power.

✚ The right pile adjustment is important, too. 1) Set the brush to its highest setting, completely clear of the floor, and turn the vacuum on. 2) Lower the nose (beater bar) until you hear it just come in light contact with the carpet—that's the setting you want. If you set it too low ("I'm really gonna dig out that dirt"), you cut off the air flow and slow down the beater bar, so you can't clean efficiently.

✚ Is the beater bar belt on correctly? (See the guide notch on your machine.) Does it need replacing? A worn belt is almost as bad as a broken one!

✚ If the belt is running hot, clean the motor pulley with kerosene or paint thinner to remove the glaze (carpet thread can lacquer the pulley).

✚ Are the bristles on the beater bar or brush roll long, strong, and

147

full? If not, slip in a new brush insert—it's easy.

Check the beater occasionally for cracks or jagged edges that can snag carpet pile.

+ The easy-clean fan chamber opens up quickly for removal of accumulated debris. If the fan has broken "teeth," replace it, because you're losing suction.

+ To avoid leaks, keep the bag clip tight.

+ Never run over the cord or let it be pinched in doorways.

+ Avoid using extension cords, they lower your vacuum's performance.

+ Wind the cord on the loops after each use, to keep it from getting twisted and tangled.

+ Keep the handle clean. It's easier to grip and healthier too.

+ Check every once in a while to see that the handle is tightened down.

+ And that the sole plate is on tight.

+ Is your machine CLEAN?. A vacuum that looks like a dirt clod on wheels doesn't do much to convince people that we clean.

Report all vacuum problems to your supervisor. DON'T attempt to repair electrical components or splice the power cord yourself unless you're skilled or trained. DO attach a note to the machine that details the problem and leave it in your janitor closet.

INTERIM carpet care

For years, our home and even professional approach to carpet care was to use it, vacuum it, use it, and vacuum it, until the carpet got heavily soiled. Then shampoo it, and repeat the process for the life of the carpet. This is now called restorative cleaning, and to head off the need for it we've added a middle stage of carpet care called interim cleaning. We do this as soon as the carpet gets lightly soiled, before it has a chance to get really bad. It's like getting a flu shot before you ever feel the flu coming on. We use the interim system in bathrooms, lobbies, and churches, especially, to keep them looking new and fresh every day.

Interim cleaning can be done several different ways, one of which is the Bonnet System.

BONNETING

The Bonnet System is a surface-cleaning procedure in which the carpet is wiped or rubbed clean with a heavy cloth "bonnet" or terry towel. It's not to be mistaken for a carpet deep-cleaning operation. It's a carpet maintenance technique intended to never let carpet get to the point of needing a major shampooing. It removes the sticky dirt that accumulates on the top or face of the carpet. The bonnet system is used by most progressive commercial companies, and can easily be adapted to most situations.

The "Bonnet Treatment" is fast, easy, and inexpensive. It will delay or preclude shampooing and keep the surface of the carpet fresh and clean. It does take a good schedule to produce the best results. For heavy-use areas like halls and offices, bonneting might need to be done once a week. Elsewhere, once a month should do it. Bonneting can damage carpet fiber if done too often or too heavily.

What to use

You can use your regular floor machine with a round bonnet pad. Or purchase an oscillating machine (much more efficient and easier to use).

How to do it

The process is simple. A cotton disc or carpet bonnet is moistened with carpet cleaning solution and wrung out in your mop bucket. Then it is mounted under a floor polisher or oscillating machine and run over the carpet. Bonneting can also can be done by hand.

Spray the carpet ahead of the machine with a spray bottle or pump sprayer to keep it moist. The bonnet will pick up and absorb surface grime and soils. When the bonnet becomes dirty, turn it over and repeat the process. When both sides are dirty, rinse the bonnet clean, wring and repeat.

The bonnet system can keep carpets at a consistent level of cleanliness and replace the old inefficient up-and-down approach to cleaning. Its biggest downfall is soap residue left behind, which causes resoiling. A good extraction cleaning is needed after long periods of bonneting. Using a good soil retardant shampoo for your bonneting solution will reduce the soap residue problem.

A pro look at
DEEP CLEANING
of carpet, or "shampooing"

Eventually, and many times in its life, carpet will get this "bath" or deep cleaning in an attempt to remove all heavy and ground-in soil. There are six basic (major different) methods or approaches for getting this job done. Which is best? Well, if any of them were perfect, the other five probably wouldn't exist. And some carpet manufacturers do require that certain methods be used, or the warranty will be voided. In other words, you have a choice and trust me, if you want to learn more about a particular way or how to do it, just call a salesperson, he or she will teach you fast!

Drying time, availability, and the soil load are also major considerations in the decision as to which deep cleaning method to use.

Dry cleaning

Solvent-impregnated powder is spread on the carpet, and then worked into it. The soil deep in the carpet is absorbed by the powder (it turns dark), then it's vacuumed up.

Dry foam

This is kind of like the foam you get from a can of shaving cream, but it's generated by machine. It's spread on and worked in with a brush, and then the dirty foam is pulled out of the carpet by a vacuum designed for that purpose.

Rotary/wet-dry

This is the oldest method of carpet deep cleaning. You apply the solution, buff with shampoo tank/brush, and then pull the dirty solution out immediately with a powerful wet/dry vac or extractor. Some machines do these two operations in one pass.

Extraction (or "steam cleaning")

A popular method often erroneously called "steam cleaning." Extraction units of all sizes are available and they spray solution into the carpet, then suck it right back out. This is all done in a single process by a single spray head.

This method can be combined with the rotary method.

Steam

True steam cleaning involves a large (often truck-mounted) unit that shoots heated water into the carpet in a heavy PSI saturation. Then it extracts the water and dirt immediately, recovering most of the moisture.

Is it time?

There are several ways to tell when shampooing is needed.

1. Carpet is matted and sticky.

2. Compare with a saved remnant of the carpet. Many carpets soil and darken so gradually we hardly realize it's happening. (Remember of course, that every carpet loses some color by fading, age, and daily wear and tear).

3. You can see grimy three-foot circles around the desks and chairs.

4. A dust storm develops when you walk across it!

Remember, when you start noticing that the carpets look bad, it's too late!

PRO SHAMPOOING SECRETS

■ *Always pre-spray* This is like prespotting a dirty collar or stain before laundering. A quick light pre-spray of a specially designed solvent on heavily soiled areas of the carpet will dissolve much of the surface dirt and grime and save lots of scrubbing.

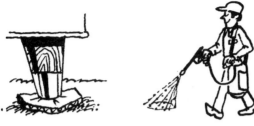

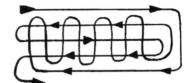

■ *Always block furniture legs* to protect both them and the carpet. Use a piece of wax paper or cardboard. If an imprint remains after you remove it, rub with a bit of clear water on a cloth. Brush the area up and let it dry.

■ When you're doing **rotary shampooing**, you usually want to cover about a 5' x 5' area at a time, with the machine releasing enough shampoo to create a foam. Go over the area twice or more, in opposite directions each time.

Then immediately extract/rinse with hot water.

The Professional Approach to

SPOTS, SPILLS, AND STAINS

During my first 15 years as a pro cleaner, spot removal was so minor, it hardly mattered. Then with wall-to-wall carpet came wall-to-wall stains. Now we had carpet on everything—stairs, garages, halls, gyms, classrooms, even in the cafeteria (the spill capital of the world). Next came the fast food industry and all that convenient take-out food—taken out of their buildings and into ours! As a result stain removal is a major time consumer in cleaning today (as much as 20% of our time goes to it).

TWO BIG TRUTHS ABOUT STAINS

1. Stains are ugly. They really cut the image of clean. If one stain is missed, an otherwise entirely clean building can be reduced to zero customer satisfaction.

2. Removing stains takes time. Stains won't pop out, we have to work them out. Identifying and effectively removing them takes training and knowledge.

There is no simple solution to spots and stains, they're complex, or as one Chicago rug cleaner told me during a radio broadcast, "There aren't any heroes in spot and stain removal." Right! And we cleaners above all know there's no miracle removal out there.

You have to know how to handle spots if you're going to be a real professional. If you have lots of stain problems buy a kit with 12 different solvents and removers. Then school yourself, attend seminars, study and learn the full art of stain removal. If spotting is just a small part or occasional or part of your job, stick to a 3-solution kit and learn the basics of guerilla spotting.

151

Your job here has two parts: Not just Removal, but PREVENTION!

PREVENTION

If stains don't occur, you won't have to worry about them. And you CAN help prevent them!

- Keep good mats in critical catch-all areas!
- Use soil retardants whenever possible.
- Use sealer on wood and concrete to keep stains out.
- Control the circulation and disposal of food and drink
- Police and remove spillables before they spill!
- Provide easy access to cleaning tools so "spillers" can clean it right up.
- Have extra protection and covers (mats, tarps) for potentially messy special occasions.

REMOVAL

1. Act fast and catch it while it's fresh; chances for removal are 75% better. Remember: a spot is ON, a stain is IN!

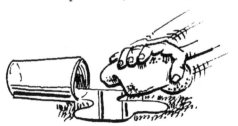

2. Do all you can to identify the stain before you start: a) look b) smell c) ask d) touch (but don't taste).

3. First blot up all the liquid and scrape up all the solids you can. A bone or plastic scraper is good for this and easy to carry right on you at all times. On a large liquid spill you can use a wet/dry vacuum. Be careful not to spread the stain.

4. Use white cloths for stain removal. This tells you a) if the item is colorfast b) if the stain is coming out!

5. Pre-test any chemical you intend to use in a hidden area to make sure it won't discolor, damage, or dissolve the surface!

6. Apply the recommended spotter and work from the outside of the stain toward the inside, to avoid spreading the stain. Blot, don't scrub; strike with the flat face of a spotting brush if necessary to help break up the stain.

7. If it's a mystery stain, first try a dry solvent. It's still there then try a water-based spot remover.

8. Rinse chemical spotters out with water, blot the area dry and feather the edges. Brush or fluff up pile or nap.

9. On carpet and upholstery, put a thick pad of toweling over the spot, weight it down with a heavy object, and leave it there for several hours to "wick up" any remaining moisture or stain residue that may still be there deep down.

BASIC SPOT SUMMARY

This is a basic chart of "Dissolvers" I use to be sure I'm using the right solvent on the right stain. Some stains do require a combination of chemicals and a several-stage attack.

For a good general background in stain removal and a great reference book, I recommend *The Stainbuster's Bible*. For a copy send $10.00 plus $2.50 for postage and handling to:

Stainbuster's Bible
PO Box 700
Pocatello, ID 83204

DRY SOLVENT	ACID SPOTTER (includes most vegetable and plant stains)	ALKALINE SPOTTER (includes most stains of animal origin)
lipstick		
mascara		
rouge		protein
other cosmetics	mustard	blood
shoe polish	grass	sweat
nail polish	soft drinks	urine
lacquer	fruit juice	vomit
enamel	wine	animal or human waste
airplane glue	whiskey	body discharges
ink	medicine	albumin
paint	coffee	egg
varnish	tea	other foods
tar	soy sauce	milk
oil	steak sauce	starch
carbon	cherry pie	sweets
crayons	tree bark	glue
pencil	chocolate	beer
wax	mud	red dye
smoke stains	tannin	ice cream

153

HOW TO DO IT:
FLOORS
The image builder
or breaker

OUR FLOOR GOALS

Beauty—we want to keep them clean and attractive.

Safety—keep them nonslippery.

Protection—maintaining a floor well means protecting it from abrasion.

Cleanability—any dirt that lands there should be ON the floor, not IN it.

The appearance of the FLOORS contributes more to the overall image of a place than any other single thing. The floor can make the whole place appear clean or dirty. Floor care is not a list of equipment, products, rules, and systems. It's simply maintaining a surface to keep it attractive and safe, and so that dirt and marks can be cleaned off easily and the finish revived easily when it needs to be.

Our standard is that **all floors be free of dirt, debris, spills, and stains at all times.**

This includes corners and edges, and door thresholds, where dirt has a tendency to build up. These areas and baseboards as well must look sharp and clean.

Thirty books could be written on the various floor surfaces and possible finishes and their care, so we can't cover the full course in just a few pages. But with the basic knowledge here, along with some brains and biceps, you can achieve one of the most valuable positions in pro cleaning—being a good floor person. This is an envied area of expertise. So whenever you have a chance, learn, watch, and attend seminars to increase your knowledge of floor care.

Some common HARD FLOOR types and their maintenance

Sheet Vinyl and Vinyl Tile (resilient flooring)

All resilient floors, even "no wax" floors, must have a coat of protective finish or "wax" so grit from foot traffic won't wear or damage them. Keep floors like this dust mopped or swept regularly (even if you can't see anything on them). When soiled, damp mop with a light solution of neutral cleaner. Scrub and refinish or touch up finish in areas of wear as needed.

Some floors are much easier to maintain than others. Differences in texture, color, quality, and age all contribute, so don't stress yourself out trying to match the bank lobby shine!

Wood

Keep wood floors covered with a protective varnish, urethane, or other resinous floor finish. If wood floors have a "seal coating" like this moisture and stains can't penetrate the wood. A little bit of water won't hurt wood if it doesn't penetrate it. When moisture penetrates wood it swells and cracks it, and causes the finish to blister and peel.

Treat well sealed wood floors like any other hard floor except go easy on the water—don't flood it and don't leave any moisture on there long.

Concrete

Concrete will bleed dust off with use and during the sweeping process. Interior concrete more than 28 days old should be cleaned thoroughly, dried, and then sealed with a resinous or acrylic concrete seal. The resulting tight shiny finish makes concrete easy to dust mop, damp mop, and maintain just like other floors. It protects the floor from stains too. I don't paint concrete floors. When paint starts to chip and scratch, it looks tacky. Clear seal looks best and is easier to touch up. You might have to sell your superiors on seal—do it!

Earth tile/ceramic tile/terrazzo

Glazed ceramic tile needs no finish, you just have to put a penetrating masonry sealer on the grout to keep it from staining and discoloring. Regular sweeping and mopping and an occasional machine scrub will keep glazed floors bright and shiny. Use only neutral cleaner, and not too much of it, to avoid a dulling soap film when you mop.

Raw "quarry" tile is quite durable and functional with just a penetrating masonry sealer on it, but it will be dull and perhaps dry looking. To achieve a low gloss and depth of color, mop with Murphy's Oil Soap and buff when dry with a buffing brush or white nylon buffing pad. Getting a high gloss finish on quarry tile is a complicated and time-consuming process that is not advisable even if possible!

Remember !

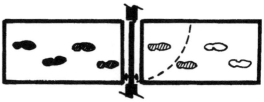

Good walkoff mats at all entrances will save more work and keep floors looking better than all the gimmick tools and magic chemical formulas combined. Then sweep and mop according to the dirt load and the work schedule to keep damaging grit and sand from grinding into the floor as people walk on it. Mop up spills or tracked-in water immediately. Barricade any wet, slippery floor surfaces with "Wet Floor" signs, and wear rubber-soled shoes to avoid slips and falls when mopping, scrubbing, or waxing floors.

155

Daily floor care...

Sweeping

Sweeping means removing dust and loose dirt and debris. Careful sweeping will pay big dividends in reduced scrubbing and waxing, as well as improved appearance and safety (dusty floors are slippery). Floors need daily sweeping.

Use a fine-bristled push broom for sweeping tile floors with rough grout. Stiff-bristled nylon push brooms are for outside or heavier sweeping.

A dustmop is the fastest, most effective sweeping tool for smooth surfaces. Use the swivel head type and always match size to use—18" for congested areas, 24" for general sweeping, 36" or 48" for wide open spaces.

If you have a lot of stairs to deal with a backpack vacuum is the best way to "sweep."

What you need

1. dustmop or broom

2. hand broom and dust pan

3. a putty knife to scrape up gum or tar

How to do it

1. In aisles and corridors a straight end-to-end sweeping method is best. In open areas dust mop in a side-to-side pattern with the same edge of the mop always leading, and never lift the mop off the floor. A dust mop is light and mobile enough to operate one-handed so the other hand is free to move chairs, and other objects. This will increase your production 40%! Hold the mop in your right hand, move furniture with your left, and work from right to left for greatest efficiency.

2. Use your hand broom to clean out corners, behind furnishings, and floor edges.

3. As you accumulate dirt, sweep it into a pile (not a long row), and use your hand broom to sweep it into the dust pan and dispose of it. I like small portable dust pans and foxtail pickup brooms or "counter brushes."

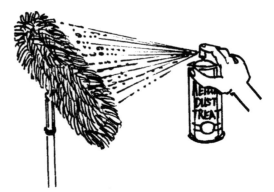

4. Dust mops should be brushed out after use and lightly re-treated with dust mop treat. Change heads as needed. After washing, dust mop heads should be sprayed with dust mop treat and placed in a plastic bag for 24 hours to reabsorb treatment before using. Rental dust mops come ready to use. Never store dust mops on the floor or against walls, or the surface will suck the oil treatment out of the mop and make a stain.

When sweeping doesn't clean it...

Damp mopping

Even the best sweeper and the best broom or dust mop still leaves the dirt that's stuck to the floor, but damp mopping will get all that.

What you need

1. "Wet Floor" signs

2. mop bucket (3" casters are best) with wringer, half filled with neutral floor cleaner solution

3. empty bucket and wringer

4. mop (I like a 24 oz. head)

How to do it

1. SAFETY FIRST! Before you do anything else, mark the area well with "Wet Floor" signs.

2. Be sure the floor has been swept, dust mopped, or vacuumed well before applying water, and move any furniture, etc., you can out of the way.

3. Now get the mop bucket half-filled with cleaning solution and an empty bucket into which you wring the dirty water. Dip the mop into the solution bucket, and wring it out almost dry. (When you wring watch the mop handle so you don't break anything, such as a light fixture overhead.)

4. The way we mop is a lot like coloring with crayons—outline the area first and then fill in the middle. Run the mop all around the outside of the room or area in one continuous stroke. Then use a figure "8" pattern to fill in the middle.

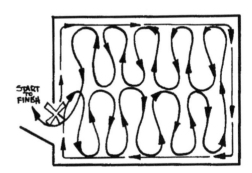

Outlining first prevents water from being slopped up onto the walls and the figure 8 helps make sure that every bit of floor is gone over twice. The first stroke

wets the surface and dissolves the dirt, and the overlapping stroke picks up the loosened dirt. This pattern covers an arm's span of floor at a time, so you can complete each section without walking. Move backwards as you mop, working from the back of the room to the front.

5. When the mop is dirty on one side, flop it over to the clean side. When both sides are dirty wring the dirty water out into the empty bucket. Don't dip a dirty mop into the cleaning solution without wringing it first, or the solution will quickly turn muddy and ineffective.

6. Keep your mop water clean. Change it as often as needed. You should be able to see a quarter dropped in the bottom of the bucket—if you can't, the water needs changing! If you see a film or mop streaks on the floor after it dries, you're either using too much chemical in the water or mopping with dirty water.

Clean your bucket, wringer and mop thoroughly at the end of each shift and store your mop so that it will air dry, preventing sour odors.

When damp mopping doesn't clean it . . .

Spray buffing or burnishing

A process of removing black marks, scuffs, and finish blemishes from waxed floors without rewaxing. You use a buffer for spray buffing, and when a mark or scuff or dirty area appears, you shoot a mist of spray buff solution. The solution moistens the dirty surface area and then the pad comes along and peels up and collects the crud and leaves most of the surface intact and glossy.

Spray buffing also tends to harden the finish for better appearance and greater soil resistance. Spray buffing is usually done 1 to 3 times per week depending on traffic.

Burnishing is a similar process, but is done with a high-speed machine and no spray. Modern thermoplastic floor finishes have been designed to respond well to the heat generated by burnishing. A mop-on finish restorer can be used for burnishing.

What You Need

1. Spray bottle or pump sprayer with spray buff solution—buy premixed or mix 1/2 gallon water with 1/2 gallon wax and add a teaspoon of APC

2. 16-20" buffer (drive pad with nylon bristles is best),

3. Synthetic buffing pad (red is most common)

How to do it

1. First, sweep or dust mop the floor; damp mop as necessary to remove spills or adhered soil.

2. Lightly mist the traffic area with spray buff solution—it's important to use as little solution as possible to avoid wax buildup in the pad. Don't spray solution on edges or on furniture as it will build up and look bad; keep it only on the traffic area.

3. Buff over the misted area with the pad—one pass will usually dry the floor and leave it dull and smeared looking; a second pass will polish it and leave it smooth and shiny. If it takes more than one pass to dry, you're using too much spray.

4. To remove black marks, it may be necessary to use a little extra solution and "heel" the machine on the mark to increase pad pressure. If it remains, scrub off the black mark with a green scrub pad, being careful not to take off too much finish! Then spray with solution and buff.

5. After spray buffing, dust mop to remove any fine powdery residue left on the floor.

6. Tilt machine back on handle to remove used brush or pad and place in plastic liner to transport to janitor sink. Clean brushes and pads immediately after use—before they dry. Run under hot water in the janitor sink. Let dry.

When spray buffing doesn't clean it...

SCRUBBING

When spray buffing or burnishing isn't removing the black marks, or impregnated dirt is making the finish look dull and dingy, it's time to scrub. Wet scrubbing removes one or more layers of finish, depending on how aggressively you do it, and leaves the floor clean and ready to recoat with finish. Scrubbing is much less time-consuming than stripping, and should be done whenever the floor can't be kept at an acceptable standard by sweeping, mopping, and spray buffing or burnishing.

For scrubbing you want to use a light cleaner, so it won't cut the wax or finish. A neutral cleaner is best.

Scrubbing is a two-person job.

What You Need

1. Mop and mop bucket with light solution of APC, 1/2 cup to 2 gallons water (don't use harsh alkaline cleaners that will soften the finish)

2. Floor machine

3. Green or blue floor machine pad, and red pad

4. Long-handled floor scrubber with blue pad

5. Mop bucket with rinse water and rinse mop

6. Mop bucket with wax and wax mop

How to do it

1. First, sweep or dust mop the floor.

2. Dip mop in APC solution and wring

out lightly. Mop a thin coat of solution over about a 200-300 square foot area, small enough that it won't dry on you.

3. Scrub traffic areas with the buffer—hand-scrub edges only as needed to remove adhered soil and "corner crud."

4. Pick up scrub water with mop or wet/dry vac and rinse with clean water.

5. The floor is now clean but it will appear dull or cloudy. When floor is dry, buff with a red pad to remove residue and bring the shine back.

6. Dust mop thoroughly.

7. Re-apply finish in traffic areas as necessary.

8. Next day, spray buff to harden new finish and blend in edges for uniform appearance.

Buffer Safety Basics

• When working with a floor machine, keep both hands on the handle.

• Tilt the machine back on its wheels and straddle the handle to attach a brush or pad to the bottom. Never place a brush under the machine and lock it into place by running the buffer onto it; always put brushes on the drive block by hand.

• Never leave a buffer unattended, and always unplug it when it's not in use.

When scrubbing won't revive it...

STRIPPING

Or stripping and refinishing, is a floor's "full bath." When the wax is old, discolored, and built up on the edges, mopping, scrubbing, and spray buffing can't resurrect it. So we strip it or take it all off and apply a new finish.

CAUTION

Stripping isn't just costly and time consuming, it's dangerous and it rapidly depreciates a floor. Keep floors swept, mopped, and scrubbed regularly to avoid unnecessary stripping. Waxing only the traffic areas when you're rewaxing will forestall the need for stripping, too. Low wear areas (corners, edges, under furniture) will build up and yellow if you continually wax them.

Stripping is a job for two or three people.

What you need

1. Dust mop, hand broom, and dustpan

2. Scraper or putty knife

3. Four mops and wringers

4. Bucket with stripper solution (follow mixing directions on label)

5. Buffer with brown or black stripping pad. Fit size of buffer to openness or restriction of room

6. Long-handled floor scrubber with brown or black pad for edges

7. A floor squeegee and dustpan, or a wet/dry vacuum for pickup

8. Bucket with neutralizer rinse solution

9. Bucket with clear water rinse

10. Bucket with floor finish. Use a top grade one—it's cheaper in the long run.

How to do it

1. Clear area of movable contents such as desks, chairs, tables, etc. Heavy furniture may be cleaned around.

2. Dust mop area to be stripped. Remove gum and other foreign matter from the floor with putty knife or scraper.

3. Mop a generous coat of stripper over the floor, including the baseboards if they're built up with wax. Confine your work area to about 200 or 300 square feet at a time so the solution won't dry before you can pick it up.

4. Let solution remain on floor for about four to six minutes to emulsify the finish. Using a brown or black pad under the machine, start at the right hand corner and work your way across the room. When removing finish always scrub floor in both directions; this ensures cleaning of low places in uneven floors. Use long-handled floor scrubber with brown pad along edges.

5. Squeegee up the "gunk" into a puddle with a floor squeegee and scoop it up

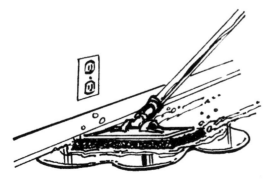

with a plastic dustpan. Or remove with wet/dry vac. Then flood-rinse floor immediately, before it can dry.

6. In your second rinse, use a floor neutralizer or 1 cup of vinegar in the rinse bucket to bring the floor back to neutral pH. This may not be necessary if using "rinseless" stripper.

7. Rinse with clear water.

8. For a top-quality job, when the floor is dry, buff with a red pad to smooth out any roughness and remove any remaining soap residue.

9. Apply new finish with a clean 16-24 oz. rayon mop or a wax applicator. Several thin coats is better than one heavy one. Cover everything lightly with the first coat; the rest of the coats go on traffic areas only, to avoid buildup on the edges.

If a floor has received hard use, you may want to apply a couple coats of sealer first after stripping and before re-waxing.

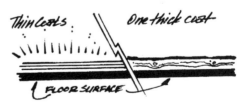

A good shine will hide a multitude of sins. Some floors need three or four coats of finish to build them up to a gloss. If the floor won't shine, or it is difficult to maintain, consider replacing it or carpeting it if the lack of shine bothers you.

HOW TO DO IT:

WINDOW/GLASS Cleaning

Windows and glass are the showpiece of our cleaning statement. To own, manage, or work in a cleaning job you have to know how to do them.

I'm ashamed, but I'll admit that I went 15 years as a pro cleaner without ever really knowing how to clean windows. I worked away at them with Bon Ami, sprays, Glass Wax, and vinegar, like tens of thousands of you are doing right now. Then one day I learned (in 20 minutes) how to clean glass.

Sprays, aerosols, waxes, rags, newspapers, and vinegar are not even fit for a home situation—they're slow, expensive, and yield ugly results. Use Windex-like sprays only for small glass areas or spotting.

What you need

1. A professional-quality brass or stainless steel squeegee from a janitorial supply store, with a 12 or 14 inch blade (or a size to fit your windows). Don't go to a supermarket or discount store and buy those reconditioned war clubs they call squeegees. They won't work well even in a professional's hands.

2. A window washing wand

3. An extension handle if you have to do high windows

4. If you do a lot of windows, a squeegee holster and belt will make things easier on both the squeegee and your back (saves bending).

5. Your window cleaning solution can be window cleaner mixed up from concentrate, or ordinary liquid dish detergent, which will work well if you use it sparingly.

PROFESSIONAL PROCEDURE
starts with
PRO EQUIPMENT

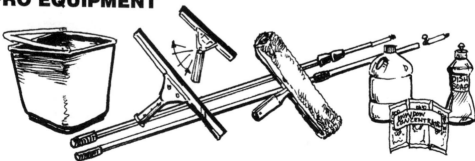

How to do it

1. Mix up the solution you're using. If you're using dish detergent, add no more than a couple of drops to a healthy bucket of warm water. Follow the directions if you're using concentrate. We're always tempted to add too much soap or detergent, which leaves residue and causes streaks.

2. Wipe around the outside edge of the window with a damp cloth to remove any debris that might otherwise get caught under your squeegee blade.

3. Dip the flat side of the window washing wand (or a sponge) just about 1/4 inch into the solution and wet the window lightly. Then go back over it to loosen any stubborn soil, and run your scrubber quickly around the window against the frame to pick up any dirt you may have shoved against it.

4. Before you start squeegeeing, wet the blade of the squeegee with a damp cloth, so it won't skip and jump around on the glass. Wipe the blade between strokes, too, while you're working with it.

5. Tilt the squeegee so that only about an inch of the blade rests lightly against the top of the window. Then pull it straight across the top to create a dry strip about an inch wide. This will prevent drops from running down from the top.

 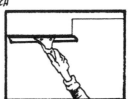

ABOUT 1" INCH

6. Put the squeegee blade in the dry area and pull it down to about 3 inches from the bottom of the window. Repeat until the whole window is done, being sure to overlap a little into the last stroke each time to keep water from running into the already clean area.

You can also quickly develop a "fan" or one-stage squeegee technique by pulling the squeegee up from one side of the bottom, across the top, and in a swinging arcing motion down the window from there. You can clean the entire window this way without lifting the squeegee off the glass.

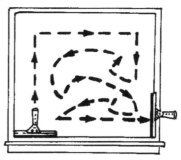

7. Run the squeegee along the bottom of the window now to remove accumulated water and wipe the sill with a dry cloth.

WHAT ABOUT DRIPS, MARKS, OR LINES?

Use your bare hand! The solution will have cut the oils in your skin by now, and you can wipe small spots without leaving a mark. As for the tiny 1/32" line of moisture at the edge, leave it! It will evaporate away unnoticed. Avoid the temptation to wipe it with a cloth or you'll end up with a 1/2 inch streak.

FOR SPOT CLEANING GLASS OR SMALL AREAS:

Use a spray bottle with an alcohol-based quick evaporating glass cleaner, and polish dry with a cloth.

WHEN SCRAPING ON WINDOWS

Make sure the razor is in a holder, then wet the surface, and scrape in one direction (forward strokes) only. Pulling a razor back and forth across the glass will trap grit under the blade and scratch the glass.

*__Avoid__ washing windows in hot/direct sunlight. They dry too fast and streak.

*__Really dirty outside windows__ should be hose-rinsed quickly first, to remove the rough stuff (mud, cobwebs, bird bombs, etc.) before washing.

*__Hard water deposits__ on windows can be removed with restroom acid cleaner (unless they've been accumulating so long that they're etched into the glass).

*For __high windows__ use an extension handle (models that extend from 4-8 or 8-16 feet are available). A squeegee with a swivel blade assembly allows you to remain in a stationary position and decreases risk. Tap the pole after each squeegee stroke.

*__Plexiglas:__ Scratches super easy. So rinse every bit of dust and grit off the surface first, and then use a soft cloth and special Plexiglas cleaner.

*Consider contracting __periodical or seasonal windows__ out to a specialist. They will do it on call, furnish the equipment, and keep your Worker's Compensation rate down.

BLINDS

Usually found in older facilities, horizontal blinds need to be cleaned often, because of their dirt-catching construction and their location. (Windows get a lot of handling and attract dirt, moisture, and bugs from everywhere!)

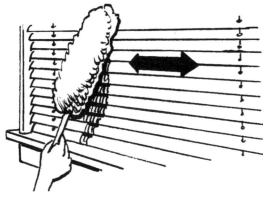

Dusting

Dust often to head off the need for deep cleaning. It will prevent dust from combining with airborne grease into a tough grimy coating. Close the blinds first, and run a lambswool duster over them, making good contact with the surface. The close them the other way and do the other side.

A lambswool duster works well on vertical blinds, too.

Cloth-covered blinds should be dusted with a vacuum dust brush.

Washing

Over time cigarette smoke, airborne grease and dust, dirty fingerprints, moisture from condensation, fly spray etc., combine into a stubborn film that must be washed off.

I'm still of the opinion that when you consider the time, money, and quality of the job, hand cleaning blinds beats ultrasonic blind cleaning by far.

Vertical blinds can be washed quickly with a tongs-like device called a Tricket.

You can do an effective job of hand washing horizontal blinds as follows.

1. Don't even attempt to wash blinds in place. Find a place, outdoors or in, where you have room and drainage for wet cleaning and hose spraying. A slanted surface is best.

2. Put down a covering on it to protect the blinds—a thick tarp, heavy quilt, or piece of carpet.

3. Get a bucket full of ammonia solution or degreaser solution, and a soft-bristled brush. An old worn out 24" push broom head, cut in half, is ideal for this.

4. Draw the blind all the way up, remove it from the window mounts, wrap the sash cords around the ends, and transport the blind to the cleaning area.

5. Let the blind out to full length, adjust the slats to vertical, and lay it gently on the cushioned surface.

6. Dip the brush into the solution and scrub the blind, making your strokes lengthwise on the slats. Then run up and down the ribbons, using a light sprinkle of a bleaching cleanser on them if they're bad.

7. Flip the blind over and do the same on the other side.

8. Then hang the blind up, hose it down heavily on both sides, and let it drip dry. If the ribbons are cloth, weight the blind while it dries with a 5-pound object of some kind to prevent shrinking.

HOW TO DO IT:

RESTROOMS

(A good janitor's final trial)

Aha... the toilet zone, the unwritten but universally accepted ultimate test of a maintenance person's mettle. Here, in this liquid-bathed land of 60 percent of cleaning complaints, few compliments, and the favorite target for vandalism and graffiti, your work is judged by all five senses, with smell being the final giveaway. Here,

brothers and sisters of sanitation, whether you are a real or novice professional is revealed. Most restrooms have the same rules, whether executive, school, or Scout camp (where you fish belts and caps out of the plumbing). I've even cleaned the restrooms in the famous Sun Valley ski resorts, as member of the "Bowl Patrol," and the same was true there.

Complete user satisfaction is our watchword here.

Some "water closet" wisdom before you care and clean:

PREVENTION of restroom problems saves time in the toilet!

■ Eliminate abrasive powdered cleansers from your cleaning program.

■ Use white nylon scrub pads—not the dark ones (black or green)—for the fixtures.

■ Avoid strongly scented deodorizers or cleaners that just mask or hide odors caused by germs. Use germicidal or disinfectant cleaners to kill the germs that cause odors.

■ Keep restrooms on a daily cleaning schedule (or even more frequent, if use is heavy enough to call for it). You seldom see restroom rankness, and by the time you can smell it, it's too late!

■ Always close or post restrooms while you are cleaning them.

If you're in there cleaning and the opposite sex opens the door, say "janitor/ custodian cleaning." Saves some shocked looks.

■ If you keep plenty of supplies on hand and keep the dispensers working, you'll keep people happier and have less mess.

■ Nowhere in the realm of cleaning are rubber gloves as reasonable as in a restroom. Use them. And when you're working with bowl cleaner, use safety glasses too.

■ Restrooms are the leader in lost and found. You'll find lots of things (watches, earrings, wallets, books, razors, bras, bottles, bodies) left lying around, so tag them, report them, and return them fast.

■ Never leave or store your own chemicals or supplies in a restroom.

Organize to sanitize

The average restroom takes three minutes per fixture, or one person can service restroom at 500 square feet per hour. That means a restroom of 250 square feet can be cleaned in 1/2 hour if you hustle.

Set up a hand carrier such as a cleaning caddy for small or few restrooms, and a well equipped cart for serious (or a siege of) restroom cleaning.

Restrooms are best cleaned by a single individual (not a group), this pinpoints pride and responsibility.

What you need

1. A mop bucket half filled with disinfectant cleaner solution

2. A mop wringer and mop

3. Two or three cleaning cloths

4. A white nylon scrub pad or scrub sponge

5. A spray bottle with disinfectant cleaner diluted according to label directions

6. A spray bottle of window cleaner

7. A toilet swab and bottle of toilet bowl cleaner

8. A pumice stone for the toilet

9. A dust mop or broom

10. A hand broom and dustpan

11. Liquid hand soap (for dispensers) or bars of soap

12. Ample supply of toilet tissue, hand towels, and sanitary napkins

13. Replacement liners for waste containers

14. Warning signs: "Wet Floor" or "Restroom Closed for Cleaning"

In cleaning any restroom, follow a basic pattern:

If possible, always work clockwise around the room.

Always bring dust and debris forward, from the back to the front, so you're always working from a cleaned area into a dirty one.

Clean nicest to grossest—sinks to urinals, in this order:

Trash and receptacles/sinks, counters, mirrors/sweep floor/spot cleaning and partitions/toilets and urinals/mop floor.

BEFORE YOU START

Make sure the room is unoccupied, and announce yourself. Place a warning sign in the doorway as a precaution.

Trash first

Empty all wastebaskets and napkin disposal cans, replacing torn or soiled liners and washing wastebaskets as necessary. Dump all ashtrays and soak or wipe away deposits as necessary.

Dispensers

Check all towel dispensers, toilet paper holders, and soap dispensers and refill as necessary.

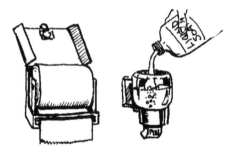

Sink area

We use our spray bottle of disinfectant cleaner to clean EVERYTHING in the restroom except the mirror, and this includes the sinks! We don't use an abrasive cleanser, such as Ajax, because it will scratch the chrome and other surfaces and eventually ruin the fixtures. We stay away from green scrub pads for the same reason—colored scrub pads are abrasive, and will scratch chrome as well as counters.

Once a spray bottle is filled with water and disinfectant cleaner in the correct proportion, the only other tools you need are a cleaning cloth or towel and a two-sided scrub sponge of cellulose and white nylon mesh (for dislodging any persistent residue).

1. When sink cleaning, first spray the inside of the bowl and the faucets with disinfectant cleaner, then polish it off with a dry cloth or paper towel. It's often best to spray several sinks ahead, and let the cleaner  soften and break down soil while you work on the first one. This loosens the soil so it wipes off easily. Use the white scrub pad to loosen hard-to-remove soap and scum and greasy soil.

2. Be sure to carefully wipe around the faucets and under the spout, getting all the corners and crevices clean.

3. Leave chrome free of spots or streaks, and polished to a high shine!

4. Next tackle the other surfaces in the sink area, and the mirrors. Remove litter from the countertops and wipe them with disinfectant cleaner.

5. Then wipe and buff the surfaces dry. They will sparkle with a glossy sheen.

6. Be sure to wipe any spots and splashes from the walls in the sink area, especially under the paper towel dispenser. Use your

glass cleaner on the mirrors and chrome trim. Don't forget to clean and polish the ash trays that you dumped and scoured earlier.

A shower stall or tub is cleaned just like you would a sink—only with more solution and agitation... and of course rinse cleaners and acids off well when you're done!

Don't use the same cloth to clean both urinals and sinks!

Sweep the floor

You've knocked some dust and debris to the floor in the course of your cleaning to this point. In a few moments you'll begin cleaning the toilets and urinals, and will probably dribble some water or cleaning solution on the floor in the course of that work. So now, while the floor is still dry, is the best time to sweep it.

Use your hand broom to clean out corners, behind the stools, under registers, and along the walls, and then sweep the open areas with your dust mop or broom.

Toilets

Cleaning inside the bowl

Use bowl cleaner only once a week in most toilets. That is usually more than enough to remove hard water stains and "rings." On the other days swab/brush each stool and urinal to loosen particulate matter with disinfectant cleaners and then flush the fixture.

Bowl cleaners are usually acids. Some are very powerful hydrochloric acids. These types are most often used in areas with very hard water and in older structures that have a heavy buildup of lime and minerals in their pipes which causes stains and rings in stools and urinals. Most of the bowl cleaners we use are buffered hydrochloric and phosphoric acids. These acids are much safer to use, and phosphoric acid will not damage carpet if we accidentally spill or drip it. Nevertheless, be extremely careful not to splash or drip any bowl cleaner on yourself or on floors, walls, and other surfaces as you clean. It is very corrosive, and can do serious damage to you as well as ruin fabrics, floor tiles, carpets, metal, and painted surfaces. **Use it ONLY on the inside of the toilet bowls and urinals!**

WARNING:

NEVER use a chlorinated bleach cleaner in conjunction with a hydrochloric acid bowl cleaner. A toxic gas is formed instantly, and that means hazardous to your health.

How to do it

1. First lift the seat and flush the toilet. Next, drive the water from the bowl. (You can do this by plunging with a swab about a dozen times or quickly pouring 3 or 4 gallons of water into the stool to lower the water level and expose any "ring" or stain.)

2. Hold the swab over the bowl and pour some bowl cleaner onto it. Begin by swabbing all around and under the lip of the bowl. This is one of the signs of a truly professional job, and one place an inspector usually checks with an eagle eye.

3. After you've swabbed the inside of the toilet thoroughly, go on to the next stall, and finish all the stools and urinals, leaving the acid on the stains.

4. When you've finished treating all the fixtures, go back to the first stool, scrub it again lightly to loosen the stain and flush and rinse the fixtures one by one. Be sure to use your bowl caddy to transport the acid-filled swab from fixture to fixture. That prevents drips and spills.

5. If any stain remains, it can be removed by rubbing it vigorously with a wet pumice stone.

The outside of the toilet

Like most things, we clean toilets and urinals from top to bottom.

How to do it

1. Starting with the tank (or with the metal piping on some wall-mounted toilets), spray on the disinfectant cleaner, leave it on for a couple of minutes to give it a chance to kill the germs (you can do something else while you're waiting), and then polish it off with a dry cloth or paper towel. Also spray and wipe the top of the lid at this time.

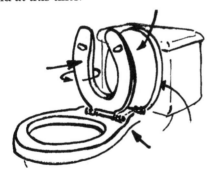

2. Next raise the lid and clean the underside of it and the top of the seat. Then raise the seat and clean the underside of it, and also around the rim and the top of the bowl. Carefully wipe behind and around the seat hinge, where dirt builds up and is hard to get at.

3. Now spray and wipe the outside of the bowl, the sides and bottom. Be sure to get clear down underneath the bowl, because drips run down the outside and collect on the bottom. If not cleaned these can be a source of bad odor.

4. Leave the seat up when you finish the bowl. This is the calling card of a cleaning professional. It says: "this toilet has been serviced by a pro, and there's nothing to hide inside." Leaving the seat up in the men's room also encourages users to leave it up unless it's needed, saving a lot of unnecessary cleaning.

5. Finish up by spot-cleaning the walls and partitions around the toilet and any spots or splashes. Be sure to give special attention to both sides of the stall doors and the push plates and handles on the restroom entry doors.
Use your disinfectant cleaner.

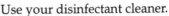

Don't forget the Doors

Doors are one of the most important parts of restrooms. Professionals never forget to clean these critical areas. Doors can be spot cleaned with a spray bottle of disinfectant cleaner (clean nightly to remove handprints). Overall dirty doors can be washed just like a wall!

Now last, Mop the floor!

You swept right after dumping the trash and filling the dispensers, before the floor was wet. Now put up your Wet Floor signs and mop the floor, using disinfectant cleaner. Some, but not all, restrooms have a floor drain. If there is one in the restrooms you clean, once a week pour about a cupful of your mop water down the drain. This kills any bacteria that might be growing there and prevents sewer gas from venting out the traps.

HOW TO DO IT:

PAINTING

When it won't clean up, looks bad, needs protection, or you just don't feel good about it... **PAINT IT!**

Rough, porous, unpainted surfaces

- Depreciate fast
- Look bad
- Are extremely difficult to clean

Painting can be a powerful ally in your cleaning efforts. I was a licensed paint contractor for years, and am convinced that a little painting wisdom can save you all kinds of maintenance woes as well as hundreds of hours of cleaning time. A coat of paint can improve cleaning efficiency up to 50%! Fingerprints, marks, dirt, moisture, can easily be cleaned off a good painted surface.

Surfaces that profit from painting:

1. Anything that will absorb and be harmed by moisture.

2. Any surface that you need to clean often.

3. Any surface you want to keep more sanitary.

4. Any surface that gets hard use.

5. Any surface you want to smooth out a little.

6. Any surface you want to decorate.

Painting is easy if you do it right

Almost anyone can be a good painter. The basic cause of the dread and discouragement painting inspires in most people is the fact that by the time you get fairly proficient in the task, it ends, and it's three or four years before you pick up the paint tools and start the learning process all over again.

Here's the secrets of those who do keep at it long enough to learn how.

BEFORE YOU BEGIN....

1. CLEAN

Paint won't stick to dirty, greasy walls. And dust, lint, and hair will get in the paint and produce "bumps." So at least vacuum before you paint... even nearby areas that won't be painted.

If the walls are greasy or very dirty, clean them prior to painting, using a good strong solution that will quickly degrease them and remove the dirt. The dry sponge is a lifesaver here 70% of the time, for walls with just ordinary soil. You can dry sponge a room down in minutes, have it ready for painting. A rented pressure washer can have dirty exterior surfaces ready to go in hours.

2. PREPARE THE AREA

Patch holes and nicks with spackle (or wood putty, for wood) and let it dry. After sanding your patch spots, coat them with shellac to seal them, to prevent dull areas in your paint job. For bare wood, follow directions on the paint can. When surfaces require preconditioning, use primer and then paint—not just two coats of paint.

Push spackle into holes tightly so that it bulges out a little, then wipe off the excess with a damp cloth.

3. PROTECT

Forget about old newspapers and flimsy plastic dropcloths. Use old sheets to cover furnishings and canvas dropcloths for the floor. They'll last for years, and you'll find many other uses for them.

Newspapers and light plastic are a poor choice for covering. Newspapers stick to your feet and won't protect from bad spills; plastic tangles and sheds dried paint droplets everywhere. Old sheets, canvas, or other cloth covers absorb drips and hold spills long enough to prevent disaster.

4. VENTILATE

It isn't heat that's needed to dry things, but air circulation. Even cool air that's circulating freely will dry paint faster than a sealed room with the heat up to 80 degrees. Breathing paint fumes reduces both your mental and physical efficiency—get plenty of air flow, it helps you *and* the paint.

5. PICK THE RIGHT PAINT

If you use a top grade washable paint, it'll be more mark and stain resistant and you won't have to paint as often. Buy well known, high quality brands. Good paint goes further, covers better, and lasts longer than the bargain cheapies. Use enamel paint for more efficient cleaning. Handprints, flyspecks, food splashes, hair oil, etc., penetrate into flat paint and often cannot be removed. I like satin enamel for surfaces that get abuse.

Choose lighter colors—let the drapes, furniture, and carpets accent your facility. Lighter colors cut lighting costs and are psychologically clean. A single color used throughout makes it easy to touch up.

How much paint will you need?

Measure the length of the walls all around the room, add together, then multiply the total by the height of the walls from floor to ceiling. Take the resulting figure to your paint dealer.

6. MAKE SURE YOU HAVE PRO-QUALITY EQUIPMENT

Good brushes and heavy-duty rollers will cover better and apply paint faster and more evenly. Ask the dealer where the professional lines are and select a nylon bristle brush—nylon lasts and keeps its spring. An angled sash brush will do a lot for your aim on trim.

I like to use to a thick furry roller cover— 3/4 to 1/2 inch pile—on most jobs because it holds more paint and covers more evenly.

Learn to use roller extension handles. They're much safer, more effective, and less tiring than painting from a ladder. They also get you back from your work so you can see what you're doing.

A deep roller pan or a bucket with screen will boost your efficiency and lessen the possibility of spills.

DO YOU HAVE?

1. Good brushes and rollers

2. Enough paint

3. Thinner of the recommended kind

4. Dropcloths

5. Spackle/putty and putty knives

6. Sandpaper

7. Masking tape

8. A sturdy stepladder

A roller screen and a 5-gallon bucket are an inexpensive, effective, and easy combination to use.

Buy professional-quality brushes. Nylon bristles last and hold their "spring."

An angled sash brush will aid your trimming accuracy.

Get ample free paint sticks.

This is one place rags come in handy.

Invest in a professional roller frame with an extension handle.

Buy professional-quality roller covers with 3/8"-1/2" nap.

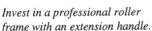

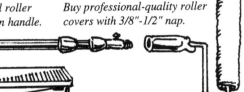

Painting secrets of the pros

Don't overdo that masking tape

Don't mask the windows and all the edges unless you're spraying several coats. Masking tape is often hard to get off, and does all too good a job of masking paint that's seeped underneath until it's too late—it's dried on there. Masking light switches, plug receptacles, and base-boards, on the other hand, does make sense and will speed you up.

Don't skimp on stirring

If your paint or varnish looks too thin right at the start, insufficient stirring is probably the reason—the heavy pigments have probably settled to the bottom. Whenever possible, have the paint store shake the paint on their machine. Don't let varnish fool you—just because it looks clear doesn't mean it's mixed.

Proper thinning may help your paint job

Solvent evaporation causes many enamel paints to get heavy when stored for long periods, or while in use. Getting paint or varnish to a flowing consistency will help achieve that smooth as silk surface you want, whether you're rolling or using a brush. Use the thinner recommended on the can and go slow—if you get it too thin you can't thicken it.

Paint in this order

When painting a room, **trim around the ceiling and woodwork first**. This will assure a neat job, and the paint you roll on later will

175

lap over the trimmed edges and they won't show. Roller paint walls next. Paint woodwork last, preferably with semi-gloss enamel. Use the paint can (with a piece of cardboard under it) for a trim bucket. Always do the baseboards last of all, because your brush (and paint) will pick up all kinds of lint and hair from the carpet or floor.

Prevent a dripping brush

Dip the bristles just halfway into the paint, then wipe the backside and bottom of the brush against the rim of the can.

Prevent "can run"

Punching a hole with a nail in the inside lip gutter of the can will eliminate "can run," and prevent paint from squirting all over when you go to reseal the can.

Don't paint too heavily

When you do, the sharp, crisp edges and corners of trim become so gobbed they make the trim look cheap and sloppy (and you can hardly tell the trim from the wall).

Roll properly

Always roll in an up and down pattern, and cross over every surface three or more times for a good looking, well distributed paint job. The first roller pass may look adequate, but there are small "pinholes" there that won't show until the paint is dry. Dip the roller in the paint, roll the excess off on the screen, then apply the roller to the wall, always going up on the

first stroke so the paint won't puddle down.

Spray painting

In the right circumstances and with the right equipment spraying is great, but not for a small job, a congested area, or a hard-to-protect one. (I once painted a large roof... and 300 cars in the lot below at the same time!). Spraying, if you do it rarely, is never as easy as it looks. Sprayers can do a 2-hour job in ten minutes, a great deal, except it took you two days to cover and tape everything and get the sprayer working.

Prep time is, however, the key of all keys to spray painting. It takes a lot of time, but it's worth it. Prepare properly and you'll spray better. Airless spray guns are great for big and fast work.

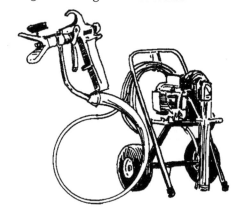

HOW TO DO IT:

GROUNDS AND EXTERIOR MAINTENANCE

Groundskeeping, or exterior cleaning and maintenance, includes:

- parking lots

- parking garages

- loading docks

- grounds lighting

- lawns

- flowers, shrubs, and trees

- sprinklers

- snow/ice removal

Most of our work is inside, but even if we don't have to do the work, we often have to supervise exterior maintenance—and a whole book could be written on groundskeeping!

A good overall standard here is simply that all areas be kept free of debris, and all greenery kept green, trimmed, and neat and attractive looking. Walks, steps, and entrances should be kept swept and free of snow and ice.

Good maintenance starts with PREVENTION

1. Provide plenty of movable, heavy duty, hard to damage and easy to clean trash receptacles.

2. Put concrete or asphalt on heavy traffic areas, and build obstructions or cut-throughs as needed to control traffic flow.

3. Fix any drainage problems.

Remember: Building entrances and lobbies are an important part of the overall feel and impression of a place, but the yard and parking lot is THE FIRST impression.

177

4. Choose plants, shrubs, and trees that are disease resistant and compatible with the area/climate.

5. Plant nothing kids can climb or walk on. Use masonry where possible.

6. Install a sprinkler system—it's a bigger labor saver than any other single grounds item.

7. Use plastic mulch and even ribbon asphalt to control weeds.

8. Buy the best commercial grounds equipment and tools.

9. Keep all blades and tools sharp.

10. Keep stuff locked up and stored right.

SAFETY

■ Keeping parking lots striped and traffic marked will prevent lots of accidents.

■ Never leave grounds tools, machines, or chemicals out or unattended. Store gasoline and chemicals in a secure place away from the main traffic areas.

■ Cover or rope off any hole or construction area.

■ Don't drive stakes and stretch support wires around the area.

■ Kids are fascinated with giant icicles—keep them off.

■ Use sterilant carefully. It can wash down and kill all the neighbor's grass and plantings.

■ Wear safety glasses, the right kind of shoes, and protective clothing when running power equipment.

■ Never work on a piece of equipment if the motor is running.

A high pressure hose is one of the fastest and best ways to clean sidewalks and concrete surfaces in warm weather. Design in plenty of spigots.

A yard vac is one of the fastest, easiest, and best ways to clean yards, walks, dirt surfaces, parking lots, etc. Picks up leaves, pine cones and needles, dirt, and litter.

When painting, remember that drips and splashes show as much or more outdoors as they do indoors. A painted blue spruce will show the yellow spot for years… so will sidewalks, railings, hardware, etc., that you might slop or spill on. So protect the area before you start and if you spill or drip, clean it off just like inside. It won't "grow away" as you might imagine!

Some ideas for SEASONAL planning/maintenance

SPRING✿✿✿✿✿✿✿✿✿✿✿✿✿✿

1. Clean up snow melt residue and litter.

2. Check all hoses, sprinklers, and irrigation units. Repair or order replacements as necessary.

3. Prune trees and bushes.

4. Repair asphalt and turf damage.

5. Reseed grass and replace dead plants.

6. Fertilize.

7. Plant flowers.

SUMMER🍎🍎🍎🍎🍎🍎🍎🍎🍎

1. Apply broad leaf weedkiller.

2. Order replacement trees for fall planting.

3. Prepare and service leaf vacuum.

4. Weed flower beds, etc.

5. Restripe parking lot.

6. Repair cement rails, fences, gates, etc.

7. Paint.

8. Kill insects and other pests.

9. Repair trash receptacles and bins and mark them.

10. Touch up or re-letter signage.

FALL🍂🍂🍂🍂🍂🍂🍂🍂🍂🍂🍂🍂🍂🍂

1. Mulch leaves on last mowing.

2. Fertilize grass and plants (if necessary.

3. Service and repair snow removal equipment.

4. Plant bulbs.

5. Service/repair/order replacements for and store lawn equipment.

6. Clean all roof/landing drains/gutters.

7. Drain and winterize sprinkler systems if necessary.

8. Remove/store things that winter weather might ruin.

WINTER❉❉❉❉❉❉❉❉❉❉❉❉❉❉

1. Overhaul, renew, sharpen all lawn equipment.

2. Remove snow and ice promptly. Use Ice Melt, not sand or salt.

3. Keep up an active outside de-littering program (pop cans kill blowers).

4. Review last year's production. See where and how you can pick up production.

5. Attend a grounds school convention and catch up on the latest.

ONCE A YEAR

■ Use weed control chemicals.
■ Replace damaged/dying trees and bushes.

AS NEEDED

■ Tighten and repair fences.
■ Replace light bulbs and repair fixtures.

Got any old or unique cleaning equipment?

Don Aslett's Cleaning Museum would like to know about it. Call or write and let us know exactly what you have—it might be perfect to add to our collection.

We're interested in commercial as well as home cleaning gear of any kind—old vacuums, mops, washers, buckets, etc.—as well as old cleaning products and chemicals still in their original packaging. Keep us in mind if you come across old ads or signs for cleaning products, old books or brochures on cleaning, or photos or stories of great moments in cleaning history, too.

The Cleaning Museum, located right here at my headquarters in Pocatello, Idaho, is rapidly becoming the biggest and best anywhere—it's attracting worldwide as well as nationwide attention. Sell or donate that old artifact to us and help raise eyebrows, teach history, and build appreciation for the second oldest profession.

Please call if you have a unique item! And if you have a snapshot, drop it in the mail so we can tell if it's something we already have. And tell us how much you're willing to part with it for or if you'll donate the item.

Don Aslett's
CLEANING MUSEUM
**PO Box 700
Pocatello ID 83204**

Quality Control Inspection Form

For General Building Cleaning
To be used monthly for each building contract.

Building _____ Floor/Area _____

Address _____ Supervisor City _____

Today's Date _____ Inspector _____

Checklist (POOR / FAIR / GOOD / EXCELL)

1. ENTRANCE
- Mats, Carpet
- Glass, Metal Surfaces
- Corners
- Floor

2. LOBBIES
- Dusting
- Floor Appearance
- Sweeping, Vacuuming
- Spot Cleaning
- Fixtures
- Water Fountains

3. ELEVATORS
- Treads
- Lights
- Walls, Doors
- Floor, Carpet

4. CORRIDORS
- Sweeping, Vacuuming
- Floor Appearance
- Baseboards
- Spot Cleaning
- Water Fountains

5. STAIRWELLS
- Rails, Walls
- Steps, Landings

6. RESTROOMS
- Dispensers, Hardware
- Sinks
- Floors
- Mirrors
- Partitions
- Toilets, Urinals
- Waste Cans
- Walls, Doors

7. OFFICE-EQUIPMENT AREAS
- Carpet Spotting
- Furniture, Equipment
- Door Kick Plates
- Phones, Lamps
- Walls, Doors, Spot Cleaning
- Glass, Metal Surfaces
- Corners
- Floor

8. RESILIENT TILE FLOOR
- Corners & Edges
- Appearance (Shine & Gloss)
- Sweeping and Mopping

9. WINDOWS
- Glass
- Frames
- Blinds

10. CAFETERIA
- Tables & Chairs
- Walls, Doors, Spot Cleaning
- Trash Containers
- Dusting
- Floor Appearance
- Baseboards
- Corners

11. JANITOR CLOSETS
- Cleanliness, Organization
- Supplies
- Equipment
- Required Manuals & Forms

12. MISCELLANEOUS
- Policing Outside
- Sidewalks
- Phone Booths
- Other _____

Quality Points Table

	POOR	BELOW STANDARD	GOOD	EXC	QUALITY POINTS
1. ENTRANCE	3.5	5	6.5	8	
2. LOBBIES	3.5	5	6.5	8	
3. ELEVATORS	1	2	3	4	
4. CORRIDORS	1	2	3	4	
5. STAIRWELLS	1	2	3	4	
6. RESTROOMS	6	9	12	16	
7. OFFICE-EQUIP AREAS	12	18	24	30	
8. RESILIENT TILE FLOOR	3.5	5	6.5	8	
9. WINDOWS	1	2	3	4	
10. CAFETERIA/LOUNGE	3	4	5	6	
11. JANITOR CLOSETS	1	2	3	4	
12. MISCELLANEOUS	1	2	3	4	
	37.5	58	78.5	100	

TOTAL QUALITY POINTS →

COMMENTS:

_____

_____

_____

Does this customer have any additional service needs?   YES ☐   NO ☐

181

10 Truths of The Cleaning Profession

The basic description of all our jobs is service in three parts: We

1
1. Know how to clean well (skill)
2. Know how to clean fast (economical)
3. Know how to keep people happy (public relations)

2
People (tenants and clients) will expect the positive and report the negative. No matter how well or how consistently you clean, customers and tenants will gradually just expect it and say nothing. But when an occasional problem arises, they'll come to life—screaming, threatening and even bullying you.

3
You can't clean well enough to please someone if they don't like you. If you hate human society, don't get along with people easily or have any obnoxiousness running in your blood, you won't last or be happy in the cleaning industry.

4
This is a lonely business. Off hours, odd shifts and low visibility means your friends and associates, although they are quality, will be limited because in this business you just aren't in circulation much.

5
This is a hands-on business—there's not much room for middle manage-ment. You can't just manipulate flunkies and peasants in the ranks. You have to know and be

able to do the work yourself to be able to boss it.

6
The biggest reason for failure in the cleaning industry is lack of commitment to the profession. Persistence and endurance are far more valuable than skill or financial backing.

7
In the cleaning field, geography makes little difference, opportunity is everywhere. Dirt is always there—in a big or little town, hot or cold climate. The carpet isn't any cleaner on the other side of the world.

8
We all hire the same people to help us clean—supervision and leader-ship are the only advantages you have over your competi-tors.

9
This is a labor-intensive business, and employee turnover is the single greatest cause of customer complaints and management stress.

10
Lack of work appreciation, not job boredom, is the biggest cause of employee dissatisfaction.

Ps. It ain't no fun if you don't make the mun.

If you have a cleaning business

(Or you're considering starting one—large or small...)

This is your chance to LEARN FROM THE LEADER

1 FULL DAY of *pure, true, solid* HOW TO DO IT information

Save years of struggle, disappointment, and heartache. Find out how to make it in the cleaning business from America's #1 Cleaning Expert, Don Aslett, owner of one of the nation's premium contract cleaning companies, Varsity Contractors.

- ☐ How to get work, bid, sell—what jobs to take, what to turn down.
- ☐ Avoiding pitfalls of partners, relatives, friends, and hiring.
- ☐ Little or big? Which is best and why. How to expand and live.
- ☐ Making money, keeping and controlling it.
- ☐ The magic of doing good work, quality control.
- ☐ Benefiting from and handling the "image" of a cleaner.
- ☐ Keeping your life and family together on the road to success.
- ☐ How much can you do? How much stuff and staff do you need?
- ☐ Facing bureaucracy, taxes, laws, and competition.
- ☐ Fun and fascination in living your clean religion.
- ☐ You'll never make it without leadership. How you can do it... well!
- ☐ Where to get help and knowledge to become better and better.
- ☐ How to turn what you know about cleaning someday into $1000 a day.

95% of cleaning businesses fail—don't you be one of them.

No frills • No fanfare • No free lunch • Just the facts!
(The handouts alone are worth the price.)

WHERE?   WHEN?
That's up to you! Don will come to your city and hold this seminar if you can find 25 people interested in attending. For more information call Don's office 208-232-6212.

Advance registration $125 ea • 2nd registrant $99
At door $150 ea (space not guaranteed)

183

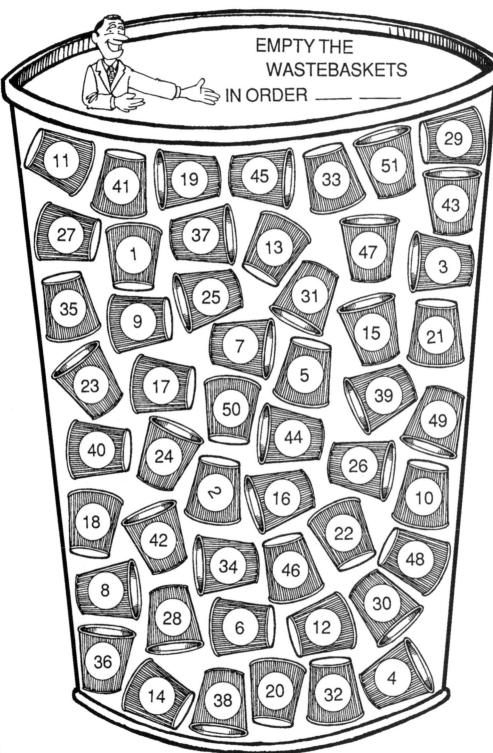

EMPTY THE WASTEBASKETS IN ORDER ___ ___

Don:

Please put my name and the following friends of mine on your mailing list for the *Clean Report* bulletin and catalog:

Name_____   Name_____

Street Address_____   Street Address_____

City ST Zip_____   City ST Zip_____

Name_____   Name_____

Street Address_____   Street Address_____

City ST Zip_____   City ST Zip_____

What would I like to see in Your Future Books?

Here's something I'd really like to see you do a book on:

Here's my own cleaning question, headache, heartache, or story, which I hope you'll mention in your next book:

_____

_____

_____

_____

_____

_____

_____

_____

_____

_____

_____

Don:
  Please put my name and the following
friends of mine on your mailing list for the
Clean Report bulletin and catalog:

Name_____   Name_____

Street Address_____   Street Address_____

City ST Zip_____   City ST Zip_____

Name_____   Name_____

Street Address_____   Street Address_____

City ST Zip_____   City ST Zip_____

What would I like to see in Your Future Books?

Here's something I'd really like to see you do a book on:

Here's my own cleaning question, headache, heartache, or story, which I hope you'll
mention in your next book:

_____

_____

_____

_____

_____

_____

_____

_____

_____

_____

_____

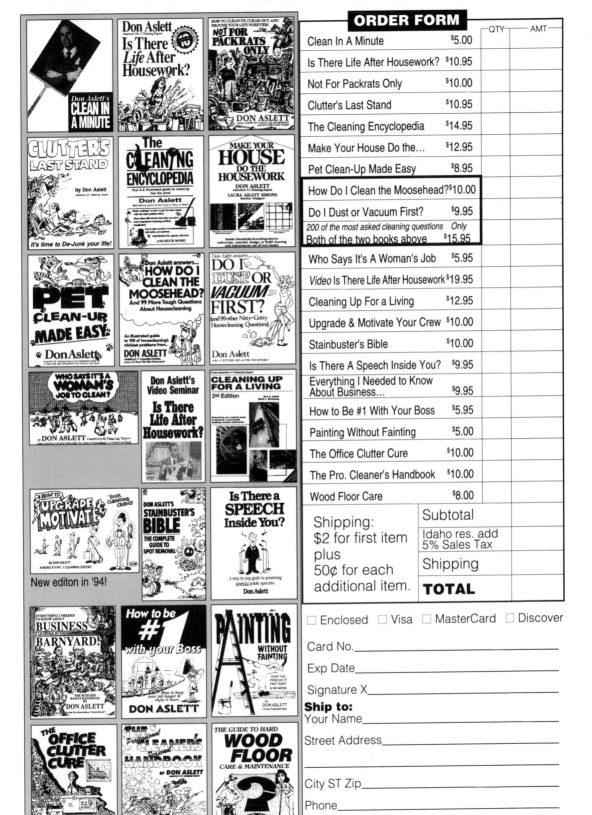

Don:

Please put my name and the following friends of mine on your mailing list for the **Clean Report** bulletin and catalog:

Name_____

Street Address_____

City ST Zip_____

Name_____

Street Address_____

City ST Zip_____

Name_____

Street Address_____

City ST Zip_____

Name_____

Street Address_____

City ST Zip_____

What would I like to see in Your Future Books?

Here's something I'd really like to see you do a book on:

Here's my own cleaning question, headache, heartache, or story, which I hope you'll mention in your next book:

_____

_____

_____

_____

_____

_____

_____

_____

_____

_____

_____

_____

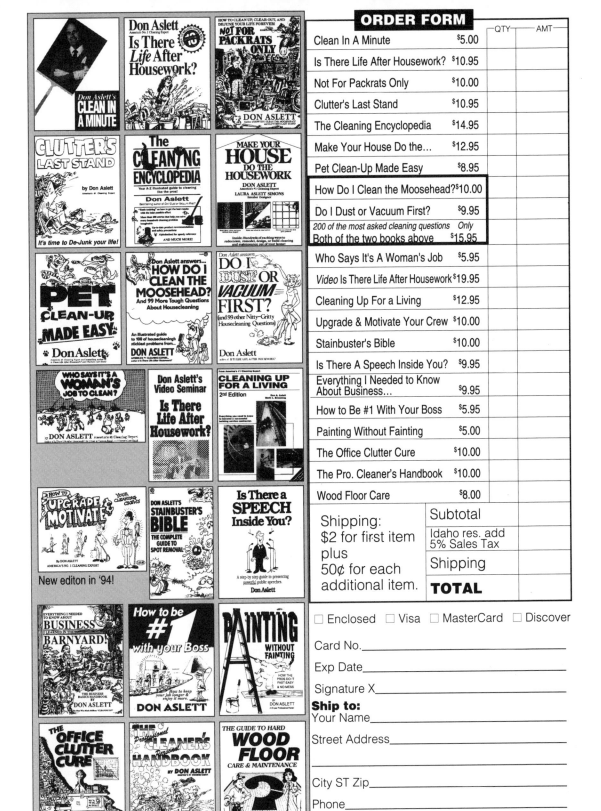

Don:

   Please put my name and the following friends of mine on your mailing list for the **Clean Report** bulletin and catalog:

Name_____   Name_____

Street Address_____   Street Address_____

City ST Zip_____   City ST Zip_____

Name_____   Name_____

Street Address_____   Street Address_____

City ST Zip_____   City ST Zip_____

What would I like to see in Your Future Books?

Here's something I'd really like to see you do a book on:

Here's my own cleaning question, headache, heartache, or story, which I hope you'll mention in your next book:

_____

_____

_____

_____

_____

_____

_____

_____

_____

_____

_____